ACTION FIGURES

of the

1980s

John Marshall

Schiffer Publishing Ltd

4880 Lower Valley Road, Atglen, PA 19310

Copyright © 1998 by John Marshall
Library of Congress Catalog Card Number: 97-80804

Book design by Blair Loughrey

ISBN: 0-7643-0494-1
Printed in China
1 2 3 4

Published by Schiffer Publishing Ltd.
4880 Lower Valley Road
Atglen, PA 19310
Phone: (610) 593-1777; Fax: (610) 593-2002
E-mail: Schifferbk@aol.com
Please write for a free catalog.
This book may be purchased from the publisher.
Please include $3.95 for shipping.
Please try your bookstore first.

We are interested in hearing from authors
with book ideas on related subjects.

TABLE OF CONTENTS

ACKNOWLEDGMENTS

Like I always say, no man is an island, and I certainly could not have pulled off this weighty tome without help.

First off, there would be no book without Scott Talis, owner of "Play With This", a collectible toy store in Pennsauken, New Jersey. Most of what you see in this book is from his store stock. He's a great source, so contact him at Pennsauken Mart, Pennsauken, New Jersey 08110 (609) 486-4556.

J. E. "Rikki" Alvarez, the world's top Transformers expert, not only loaned out his collection, but taught me everything I know—and everything you'll read—about the Transformers. There truly is more to him than meets the eye.

Additional people of great help this time around were Steven Silvia, who chipped in a few photos; Paul Levitt, the FX Channel's "Japanese Monster Maven" and chemist extraordinaire, who loaned out several of his toys; Nick Delliponti, who finds toy rarities on this and other planes of existence; Brian Savage, head of the official G.I.Joe Collector's Club; Alex Ferrer, the top 1980s G.I.Joe expert of two continents; and Fred Mahn, who wanted to contribute items for photography but was shut out by the massive scheduling we had to do. I especially want to thank my sainted mother, Janice Marshall, for letting me bum around her house long enough to finish this furshlugginer book.

And of course I must acknwowledge publisher Peter Schiffer, the Arthur Godfrey to my Julius La Rosa; editor Jeff Snyder, who took virtually all the photos in this book and who wisely doesn't edit out jokes he doesn't get; and all the gang at Schiffer who labored so mightily to bring this thing to fruition.

I want to thank my late, lamented Pop, John Marshall, for giving me my first G.I.Joe at Christmas in 1971, which started me off on my decades-long love of action figures.

It can't hurt to thank God, who endowed me with the talent to write this book, and the sensibility to use my powers for good, and never evil. Well, almost never.

Finally, I also want to thank the angelic Myrka Dellanos-Loynaz, sultry Mercedes Soler, and incomparable Maria Celeste Arrarás for the way their Spanish language news magazine program PRIMER IMPACTO brought me back to the real world every evening. After spending a ten-hour work day thinking about bizarre stories, alien invaders, and assorted strange characters, there's nothing like a dose of reality—Univision style!

INTRODUCTION

Oh, the things I do for money.

After the public enthusiastically accepted my first book, *G.I.Joe And Other Backyard Heroes* (Schiffer 1997), the general concensus at Schiffer was that I should keep writing toy books. After all, I am probably the world's expert on modern-era character collectibles. At least, I think I am. But would a book on 1980s toys have the kind of passion and involvement that the first book had? After all, I grew up in the 1970s. I was, ha ha, slightly more mature in the 1980s, and too old to play with toys. (Insert William Dozier narration here.) "Or WAS I?"

Although the 1980s were as divorced from my toy playing days as my infancy in the 1960s was, I have just as many fond memories of the toys that invaded homes while I was attending Rancocas Valley Regional High School, Sarah Lawrence College, and Brooklyn College, collectively from 1979 to 1988.

In high school, I had followed the course of Mego's decline and the arrival of Kenner's awful Star Wars figures. I had seen the astonishing and meteoric rise of Hasbro's new version of G.I.Joe and the innovation of He-Man and the Masters of the Universe. But I thought of myself as a sophisticated teenager, too old to mess around with toys anymore. However, I was still an avid comic book reader, and I did occasionally pick up a comic-related toy or get one as a present, up until I was 14 or 15.

But what happened in college was that I yearned for the simple thrill of buying a toy. And in 1984 there was no escaping all the wonderful new lines. So I broke down and started buying. G.I.Joe, Blackstar, and the monsters from Advanced Dungeons and Dragons began to fill up a shelf in my dorm room. My roomate thought it was pretty cool at first, but there got to be more and more of them, until finally I had to start taking them home just to make room. I even dated a girl whose brother was a high-up at Coleco—but not to get info on their new Sectaurs line. (Okay, not JUST to get info on their new Sectaurs line). In fact, action figures influenced my romantic relations. During more private moments with certain lady friends, I was known to utter Lion-O's famous phrase, "Thunder! Thunder! Thundercats!" at the most appropriate times.

But none of this appeal could compare to what happened in 1984, when Kenner's DC Comics Super Powers line and Mattel's Marvel Super Heroes Secret Wars line debuted. Those two series brought adult collectors into toy stores in significant numbers for the first time. Interest in collecting 1960s and 1970s action figures was just starting up, as the kids of those eras were growing up and feeling nostalgic. But Super Powers and Secret Wars provided entirely-new, available in-stores-now toy lines of interest to adults. Here were the characters popularized by Ideal, Mego, and Remco back in the old days, but in new and inexpensive incarnations.

That period began what I think of as the modern age of toy collecting, where adult action figure aficionados are just as interested as their kids are in what's on toy store shelves today. The history of action figures in the 1980s is the history of an entire cultural movement which is bigger today than ever.

As an adult, I not only appreciated and collected the toys of the 1980s—IN the 1980s—but I also love them just as much today.

So now you know, and, as they say, knowing is half the battle.

Thunder! Thunder! Thundercats! Ho!!!

How To Use This Book

Okay, look:

Essentially, this is a guide to all action figures and related accessories released between January 1980 and December 1989. Sometimes, manufacture dates and release dates are not always the same year, so I've included some temporally-marginal items like Remco's Universal Monsters, manufactured in 1979. Lines that continued into the 1990s often are listed in total, but not always. I do guarantee that you'll at least find everything made up through the end of 1989.

The chapters in this book are broken down according to the groups I have divided the items up into—in my head. You may argue that, because The Real Ghostbusters toy line was based on the characters who originally appeared in the wildly-overrated Ernie Hudson movies, that its listing belongs in the TV and Movie Characters chapter. But I say it belongs in the Real Men chapter because it's really based on the half-hour commercial spun off from the wildly-overrated Ernie Hudson movies. And what I say goes.

Since almost every major action figure line produced in this era had some kind of cartoon show or heavy media backup, I would have had to include virtually all the lines in this book in the chapter on TV and Movie Characters. What I tried to do was group the various lines according to their relationship to each other. It wasn't easy making sense of it all, but after you've read the book through, I think you'll understand my logic.

Fans of knockoffs and no-name figures will be disappointed. I only included standouts from the world of off-brands, like Remco's Warrior Beasts. A lot of the knockoff stuff is just not interesting and has absolutely no collector value anyway. Thus, if you are a fan of Flex-a-Tron or American Defense, you are spit out of luck. Unlike the 1960s and 1970s, when even the doofiest figures were of interest (then and now) the 1980s saw such a choking glut of figures that there were (and are) a large number of items that, I legitimately feel, are of no interest to anybody. And who gets to decide what's of interest to you? I do, so shut up.

Another thing you may not like is my definition of an "action figure," i.e., my determination of what

does and what does not belong in this book. Generally, an action figure has to be a three-dimensional representation of a character, designed to interact with other toys of the same kind or similar kinds, in an adventure-related, creative play scenario. That is why Starting Lineup figures are not in this book. They are figures, and generally do have a couple of points of articulation (posability), but they are really statues and are not designed to interact with each other, not designed to be "played with." Conversely, some of the items I do list, such as many Advanced Dungeons and Dragons monsters, do not pose at all, but are intended to interact with other figures to create play adventures. Does that make sense to you? If it does, you will enjoy this book immensely. If it doesn't, you will enjoy this book immensely anyway.

Generally speaking, this book only includes lines that were marketed to Americans and available in most retail stores around the country. This excludes toys like the marvelous Madelman figures, since they were available only in certain locations. This also excludes, for the most part, foreign action figure lines related to American ones from the 1980s or past decades, such as the European Big Jim lines, Japanese and European Transformers, or Britain's Action Man, the cousin of G.I.Joe. Some day I would like to do a book on these, but there are a few more years of research required to do an accurate book. However, important foreign additions to existing American lines, like South America's Super Powers Riddler, and Europe's Secret Wars Electro, Constrictor, and Iceman, are included.

How did I arrive at the prices? How accurate are they? Well, they're based on my intimate knowledge of the field of action figure collectibles. I am constantly reviewing market trends and developments, I go to shows, and I read most of the toy-market publications. Simply put, it's my job to know the relative value of any item in this book. You may notice a seeming disparity in the pricing; sometimes an item will be worth twice as much **m**int **i**n **p**ackage (MIP) as it is **l**oose (no packaging), **m**int, and **c**omplete (LMC). Other times there won't be a huge difference between the loose and packaged prices. The reason for this is that I am incompetent. Just kidding. Really, it's because some things are rare enough that they are almost as hard to obtain loose as they are to obtain in the package (The Indiana Jones figure from LJN's Temple Of Doom line comes to mind). Others, like early G.I.Joes, are just the opposite.

Some slots are marked N/A for "Not Applicable." A driver figure who came with a G.I.Joe vehicle may be listed separately because the figure has collector interest without his vehicle. But he is listed as N/A under the Mint In Package heading because he was not available separately. A Mint In Package price for the complete item (i.e. Water Moccasin with Copperhead) is provided with the listing for the entire vehicle/figure combination.

The next point will sound incomprehensible on first reading, but it conveys a simple idea. In the case of seperately-available items that were also packaged as a set, the individual figures are given a loose price and a boxed price as usual, and then a boxed gift set of the same figures is listed underneath with only a Mint In Package price. Technically, the value of the gift set loose would be the total value of the individual figures loose, but the value of the gift set Mint In Package is usually much more than the total value of each individual piece in its own package. So as not to confuse the issue, I listed gift sets in loose condition as N/A. To give an example, what is the difference between all five Transformers Stunticons sitting on a flea market table and the same figures assembled into a Menasor Stunticon sitting on a flea market table? Nothing. What's the difference between the five Stunticons in their original packages and the Menasor Gift Set in the box? Several hundred bucks.

Some listings make no logical sense upon first viewing. For instance, if a Dapol Dalek is worth $9 loose, mint, complete, why is a an eight-figure Dalek Army set loose only worth about $50? The answer is really a question of taste. Y'see, several of the Daleks in the Dalek Army playset are molded in idiotic color schemes. A Dr. Who fan looking to buy a bunch of loose Daleks would pay $9 for a nice gray job or a white Imperial Dalek, but he'd have no use for a cherry-red one. So you see, those particular Daleks are not worth $9 each. That is why you have to trust me—it's my job to know these things.

You'll see the term "pocket-size" a lot in this book. That generally means a figure that is between three and a half and four inches tall. Many publications oversimplify and call this the "3 3/4" size." But not only is that misleading, it is also a pain to type. The term "pocket size" covers things nicely. Star Wars figures, lil' G.I.Joes, and similar items are what I call "pocket size."

The price(s) in the captions reflect the value of each item as it appears in the picture, based on its completeness and condition. As a result, that price may not jibe exactly with the Loose Mint Complete or Mint In Package listing. The Mint in Package title refers to items whose packages are in reasonably good shape, but items in especially brand-new-looking packages can command even more money.

Oh, and the date that follows the name of each figure line in the price list signifies the year in which the line started.

Okay, I think that's everything. I hope you enjoy the book.

—John Marshall, October 1997 (Go Jupiter 2!)

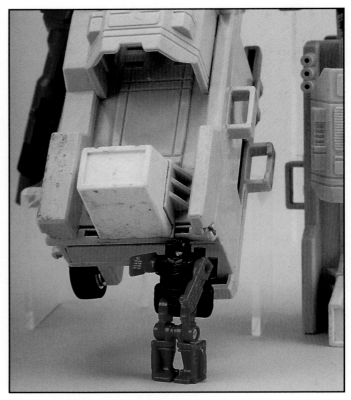

Big and small Transformers: Metroplex sneaks up on Vorath. *Courtesy of J. E. Alvarez.*

CHAPTER 1

G.I.JOE: A REAL AMERICAN HERO

Bob Prupis wanted G.I.Joe back.

The year was 1980, and Hasbro's arch-rival Kenner had revolutionized the action figure market with their pocket-sized Star Wars line. As the Marketing Director for Hasbro, Bob Prupis proposed a similarly-scaled line of World War Two heroes, recalling Hasbro's heyday as the producer of a best-selling soldier figure. "Not original enough!" declared Hasbro prez Steve Hassenfeld. But Battlin' Bob Prupis wasn't about to give up so easily.

The United States hockey victory over Russia in the 1980 Olympics was the clincher. The 1980s were obviously going to be a decade of American national pride, with an emphasis on progress and presence in the world market place. As a symbol of both cultural right and might, G.I.Joe would indeed return to his soldier roots.

In 1981, Bob Prupis continued the pitch. Supported by Research and Development commander Steve D'Aguanno and a maverick young exec named H. Kirk Bozigian, Prupis launched a new assault in an effort to bring G.I.Joe back. The new idea was for a "mobile strike force team" of modern military muscle who had great posability. (Their designs were, in fact, based on Mego's 3 3/4" C.H.i.P.s. figures). To replicate the accessorizing excitement of the old 12" G.I.Joes, the new versions were to have snap-on helmets and backpacks.

For mass media support and promotion, Hasbro's ad agency, Griffin-Bacal, had arranged for a thrilling new theme song for G.I.Joe. This stirring anthem helped win over the top brass at Hasbro. When the presentation was finished, a misty-eyed Steve Hassenfeld gave the go-ahead. What followed was an astonishing thirteen-year run for G.I.Joe, A Real American Hero.

Working with Marvel comics writer Larry Hama, Kirk Bozigian devised a series of "combat command file cards" to be included with the figures. These command files established a background and personality for each

Scarlet, the queen of the Joes, and, frankly, she's worth $30-$35. *Courtesy of Play With This.*

character that the figures represented. The result, combining a well-made figure with a fully-realized character, was irresistible. But even Hasbro couldn't think of everything. Hasbro's trade customers wanted villains, so Larry Hama created Cobra Command, a paramilitary group of modern-day corporate pirates. These baddies even had despicable bad habits like taking a bite out of each chocolate donut and putting them all back in the box!

Business-wise, G.I.Joe's marketing in the 1980s was even more carefully-considered than it was in the 1970s or 1960s. There was a fan club. There were Flag Points to save for mail-in merchandise specials. And there were also the all-powerful price points: G.I.Joe was a line that could be bought with allowance money.

The first series of Joes in 1982 was different in several respects from the ones that followed. Not realizing just how important the characters' identities were to become, Hasbro labelled each figure by its military specialty highlighted over its code name (i.e. Mortar Soldier: Codename Short Fuse and not "Short Fuse: Mortar Soldier"). Also, the figures had yet to develop their full articulation, although they were the most posable action figures on the market—heck, they had elbows! They were, for the most part, a drab-looking bunch (olive drab, that is), with many parts reused for various characters (even a few heads). Due to the popularity of the "fancier" models like the all-black ninja commando Snake-Eyes, Hasbro realized that jazzier characters could make the line more colorful, both literally and figuratively. The 1982 line also included a Sears exclusive (they were Hasbro's biggest buyer). This was the Cobra Missile Command Play Set, a cardboard affair that came with the original three Cobra Characters: Commander, Officer, and Trooper. The Commander was otherwise only available as a mail-in offer at that time.

In early 1983, the new recruits came out. All characters, including the ones introduced the previous year, now had "swivel-arm battle grip," a biceps

Carded Stalker, $90-$100.
Courtesy of Play With This.

Carded Snake-Eyes, $120-$130.
Courtesy of Play With This.

Carded Grunt, $70-$80.
Courtesy of Play With This.

joint which allowed them to hold rifles in more realistic positions. The first G.I.Joe cartoon premiered in September 1983, as a five-part miniseries that could also be broadcast as a two-hour movie. It, too, was a little reserved, just like the first toy line. But that would soon change!

By the end of 1984, the original 12 characters had been rotated out of the lineup. This rotation was to become a hallmark of the G.I.Joe line and help collectibility. As *The Revenge Of Cobra* miniseries played on TV, we got to see the coolest Joes of all arriving in stores: Roadblock, the poetry-spouting machine gunner; Spirit, the Native-American tracker; Mutt the dog trainer, complete with his dog Junkyard; and villains with real personality such as Storm Shadow, Cobra's Ninja assassin, and The Baroness, one of the first female villain figures of the 1980s.

Best of all was Zartan, evil master of disguise, who came boxed with a small Swamp Skier vehicle, an unusual format that would continue with other characters throughout the series. Zartan also pioneered the "Skin that changes color in sunlight" feature that was so popular for a while that even Albino characters had it!

Hasbro also began to issue its first "repaints"—previously released vehicles molded in new colors. The G.I.Joe VAMP jeep returned as the Cobra Stinger, complete with a gray version of the Cobra Officer as a driver.

Outside licensing became important as well, and the G.I.Joe characters found themselves on everything from bath sheets to Colorforms.

Stronger still was the output from the years 1984 and 1985, in which the G.I.Joe line reached its creative peak. This was also the era of Secret Wars and Super Powers, a time when adult action figure collecting was becoming a force in the marketplace.

Hasbro tested the big money waters with a G.I.-gantic USS FLAGG, a seven-foot, hundred-plus dollar aircraft carrier. Also around that time, Toys R Us released its exclusive "Mission: Brazil" set, featuring five repainted figures, an audio tape detailing their adventure, and an all-new figure named Claymore.

More innovations kept the line fresh. Real-life heroes entered the Joe team. Wrestling star Sergeant Slaughter was offered as a mail-in exclusive. Next, the Joe line produced one of its rarities: Zartan's sister Zarana originally had tiny earrings molded on her head, but when they proved to break off too easily, the heads were retooled without earrings. The villains at that time were being given greater emphasis, with more characters and accessories proportionally than in the early years. Cobra acquired an elite division called the Crimson Guard and there was a Crimson Guard trooper figure as well as a twin-pack of the Crimson Guard Commanders, evil twins Tomax and Xamot. Sears had a red-colored version of Joe's MOBAT motorized battle tank, and it was marketed as a Crimson Guard tank. A third TV miniseries, *Pyramid of Darkness*, was followed by a regular weekly cartoon show. The big money release of this period was a headquarters for the villains (this shows just how vital a component they were). For around

Cobraaa!!! The Commander, flanked by his Officer and a Cobra trooper, all swivel-armed, each $20-25. *Courtesy of Play With This.*

Heavy Artillery Laser with Grand Slam, $40-$50 complete. *Courtesy of Play With This.*

sixty bucks you could get the Terror Drome, a circular, rotating tower, as seen in the TV show.

G.I.Joe's best sales years were 1986 and 1987. While not as creatively inspired as the earlier series, these lines continued the emphasis on cool, colorful characters, while also attempting to expand the line with more varied and more elaborate items.

The Defiant Space Shuttle complex rivalled the USS FLAGG in size, detail, and cost; villains 'n vehicles sets continued with Zanzibar the Dreadnok pirate ("The Dreadnoks" was the name of Zartan's ever-expanding gang). William "The Refrigerator" Perry signed on as the new real-life mail-in hero, complete with football-shaped weapon. Cobra's hypnotist Crystal Ball had a file card reportedly authored by Stephen King. Hasbro also devised a Steel Brigade mail-in figure who was supplied with a command file written by the purchaser himself!

Rocky Balboa was intended to join the line at this time, but the deal was never realized. Hasbro took a look at the boxing gear they had already designed and devised Big Boa, a Cobra trainer.

At this time a separate sub-series called Battleforce 2000 was launched. This was a group of futuristic vehicles which interlocked to form a giant battle station. Special figures for this subset were also available.

The years 1988 and 1989 were poor years for G.I.Joe. Although the line was ever-expanding, the ideas were running dry. The worst aspect of this was the money-saving practice of releasing subsets featuring pre-

Whirlwind Twin Battle Gun, $30-$40 boxed. *Courtesy of Play With This.*

viously-issued items and figures in new colors, masquerading as new toys. This sad collection included Tiger Force, Night Force (Toys R Us exclusive), Slaughter's Marauders and Cobra's Python Patrol.

There were some bright spots. Destro split from Cobra to form the Iron Grenadiers, launching a new subset of figures and vehicles based on baddies. Micro-figures were included with the characters for a while, adding collectibility and interest with their miniaturized versions of popular Joes and Cobras. (They were like painted toy soldiers.) February 9, 1989 was G.I.Joe's officially-recognized 25th anniversary, and Hasbro threw a birthday party with guest Sergeant Slaughter. Strangely, Marvel's G.I.Joe anniversary comic was issued in 1988, declaring proudly "25th Anniversary 1963-1988." 25th anniversary of what?

A slight improvement was seen in 1990, but the G.I.Joe line needed a serious shot in the arm. One clever and amusing idea was EcoForce, a line of ecology-based Joes fighting the pollution powers of Cobra villain Cesspool and his "leaky suit brigade" of Toxo-Zombies, who drove around in their "Septic Tanks"! The model for Cesspool was in fact Product Manager Vinnie D'Alleva. This was a common "perk" for Hasbro execs—your face on a G.I.Joe. H. Kirk Bozigian was Law, character designer Ron Rudat was Leatherneck, and so on.

G.I.Joe marched into the 1990s with renewed vigor, and greater improvements would follow.

United Underworld presents The Baroness ($25-$30), Scrap-Iron ($18-$20), and Firefly ($22-$25). Not all accessories are shown. *Courtesy Of Play With This.*

Sayonara, sucker! If Storm Shadow's wearing all-white, it means he's on Cobra's side. Later he switched. $25-$30. *Courtesy of Play With This.*

Mutt has a slight employee relations problem with Junkyard, in a scene created by editor Jeff Snyder. $15-$18. *Courtesy of Play With This.*

G.I. JOE PRICE GUIDE 1982-1989

ITEM	LMC	MIP
Snake Eyes	$30	$125
Stalker	$25	$95
Scarlet	$30	$125
Rock 'N Roll	$22	$95
Zap	$22	$95
Breaker	$22	$95
Short Fuse	$22	$95
Grunt	$18	$80
Cobra Soldier	$35	$125
Cobra Officer	$39	$135
Cobra Commander Mail-In	$75	$95
Flak Cannon	$10	$45
Jump Jet Pack	$10	$45
Ram Motorcycle	$10	$50
Mobile Missile System w/Hawk	$45	$145
Hawk figure from MMS	$15	N/A
HAL Heavy Artillery Laser	$45	$145
Grand Slam figure from HAL	$25	N/A
VAMP Attack Jeep	$40	$140
Clutch figure from Vamp	$15	N/A
MOBAT Motorized Battle Tank	$55	$165
Steeler figure from MOBAT	$15	N/A
1983 Swivel-Arm		
Snake Eyes	$25	$100
Stalker	$20	$85
Scarlet	$25	$100
Rock 'N Roll	$20	$85
Zap	$20	$85
Breaker	$20	$85
Short Fuse	$22	$95
Grunt	$15	$70

Cobra Soldier	$30	$115
Cobra Officer	$35	$125
Doc	$15	$55
Snow Job	$16	$65
Gung Ho	$16	$65
Airborne	$15	$55
Torpedo	$16	$65
Tripwire	$16	$65
Major Bludd	$20	$80
Destro	$22	$85
Carry Case (3 figures)	$5	$25
APC Personnel Carrier	$15	$85
PAC Rat Machine Gun	$5	$18
PAC Rat Missile Launcher	$4	$15
PAC Rat Flame Thrower	$4	$15
Battle Gear Accessory Card	$10	$25
Snake Armor (White)	$14	$45
Cobra Viper Glider	$75	$195
Viper Pilot From Glider	$25	N/A
G.I. Joe Falcon Glider	$75	$195
Grunt from Glider (Tan)	$25	N/A
Jump Jet Pack w/Grand Slam	$95	$250
Grand Slam from Jump (Silver)	$75	N/A
Whirlwind Twin Battle Gun	$12	$35
Cobra FANG Copter	$5	$25
Polar Battle Bear Skimobile	$7	$30
Wolverine Tank	$50	$165
Cover Girl figure from Wolverine	$25	N/A

Cobra HISS Tank	$45	$165
HISS Driver	$15	N/A
Dragonfly Helicopter	$35	$165
Wild Bill from Dragonfly	$15	N/A
Skystriker Jet	$45	$125
Ace from Skystriker	$15	N/A
G.I.Joe Headquarters (#1)	$30	$145
Cobra Missile Command (Sears)	$225	$495
1984		
Spirit	$15	$50
Recondo	$15	$50
Storm Shadow	$30	$90
Road Block	$15	$45
Duke	$21	$69
Mutt and Junkyard	$18	$45
Ripcord	$15	$45
Blowtorch	$14	$40
Scrap Iron	$20	$55
Firefly	$25	$89
Baroness	$40	$150
Zartan w/Swamp Skier	$45	$125
Zartan from above	$25	N/A
Carry Case (12 figures)	$5	$15
Cobra CLAW	$5	$15
Bivouac	$5	$15
Watch Tower	$5	$15
Mountain Howitzer	$5	$18
Machine Gun Defense Unit	$5	$15
Mortar Defense Unit	$5	$15
Missile Defense Unit	$5	$15
Sky Hawk	$6	$22
Cobra ASP	$5	$15
Slugger Self-Propelled Cannon	$25	$64
Thunder figure from Slugger	$11	N/A
Night Attack Stinger	$25	$85
Stinger Driver (Grey Cobra)	$12	N/A
Vamp Mark 2 (Tan)	$30	$85
Clutch figure from Vamp 2 (Tan)	$15	N/A
SHARC Submarine	$25	$65
Deep Six from SHARC	$10	N/A
Hovercraft	$35	$125
Cutter from Hovercraft	$12	N/A
Water Moccasin		
(Driver has dark green gloves)	$65	$225
Copperhead driver w/ dark green gloves	$30	N/A
Water Moccasin		
(Driver has light green gloves)	$35	$95

Major Bludd and Destro, each $20-$22 with accessories. *Courtesy of Play With This.*

Above:
HISS tank with driver, $40-$45.
Courtesy of Play With This.

Left:
Cover Girl in her Wolverine tank,
$45-$50. *Courtesy of Play With This.*

Water Moccasin with Copperhead, $45-$55. *Courtesy of Play With This.*

Copperhead with light green gloves	$12	N/A	Cobra Eels	$15	$50
Rattler Cobra Plane	$65	$185	Cobra Snow Serpent	$12	$45
Wild Weasel Rattler Pilot	$10	N/A	Cobra Tele-Viper	$12	$29
Red HISS Tank w/MMS (Sears)	$45	$125	Tomax and Xamot Two-Pack	$24	$70
C.A.T. Tank (Sears)	$70	$175	SNAKE Armor (Blue)	$45	$135
VAMP Jeep w/ HAL Laser (Sears)	$85	$175	Fight Pod Trubble Bubble	$12	$25
Manta Windsurfer Mail-In	$20	$35	Weapon Transport	$4	$15
1985			Bomb Disposal	$5	$15
Bazooka	$12	$25	Cobra Night Landing Raft	$4	$15
Quick Kick	$12	$36	Cobra ASP Assault Pod	$5	$15
Footloose	$12	$30	Cobra FANG Mini-Copter	$5	$16
Barbeque	$12	$40	Armadillo Mini-Tank	$5	$15
Alpine	$12	$45	Silver Mirage Cycle	$10	$35
Dusty	$15	$48	VTOL	$7	$15
Snake Eyes 2 w/Timber	$27	$125	Cobra Ferret	$4	$15
Shipwreck	$12	$45	Battlefield Machine Gun	$4	$10
Flint	$15	$35	Battlefield Missile Defense	$5	$15
Airtight	$10	$35	Battlefield Mortar Defense	$4	$15
Lady Jaye	$22	$60	Battlefield Forward Observer	$4	$12
Buzzer Dreadnok	$12	$40	Ammo Dump	$4	$12
Ripper Dreadnok	$12	$40	Rifle Range	$4	$12
Torch Dreadnok	$15	$45	A.W.E. Striker	$22	$50
Cobra Crimson Guard	$12	$45	Crankcase Figure from AWE	$12	N/A

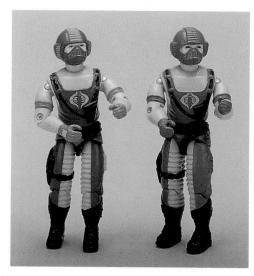

Another reason my books are worth ten times their price. Here, plain as day, are the color variations on Copperhead's gloves. Aqua green, $25-$30. Light Green highlights $10-$12. *Courtesy of Play With This.*

In like Flint: Tiger Force reissue (in brown shirt, $6-$8) with original (black shirt $12-$15). *Courtesy of Play With This.*

Zarana, with earrings, the rare one, $30-$35. *Courtesy of Play With This.*

A closeup of Zarana's earrings. There's your thirty bucks right there! *Courtesy of Play With This.*

(Homer Simpson voice)"Hmmm... Barbecue..." $10-$12. *Courtesy of Play With This.*

To bait a trap for Croc Master's gator, you'd have to be a master baitor. $10-$12. *Courtesy of Play With This.*

Secto Viper, the rarely-seen Cobra BUGG driver, $15-$18. *Courtesy of Play With This.*

Armadillo, the driver figure from the Rolling Thunder vehicle, who fools people by looking like a cheap G.I.Joe knockoff, just like a real armadillo. Or am I thinking of something else? $12-$15. *Courtesy of Play With This.*

Jinx shows her catlike moves. Still undervalued at around $10-$12. *Courtesy of Play With This.*

Snow Cat	$19	$45
Frostbite from Snow Cat	$12	N/A
Cobra Battle Bunker	$7	$22
Transportable Battle Platform	$15	$55
Cobra Hydrofoil MORAY	$22	$65
Lamprey Pilot from MORAY	$12	N/A
Mauler Motorized Tank	$25	$67
Heavy Metal from Mauler	$15	N/A
Bridge Layer Toss 'N Cross	$25	$85
Tollbooth from Bridge Layer	$12	N/A
Cobra Terror Drome w/Firebat	$95	$255
AVAC Firebat Pilot	$12	N/A
USS FLAGG Aircraft Carrier	$225	$500
Admiral from FLAGG	$12	N/A
1986		
Iceberg	$8	$22
Beachead	$8	$22
Sci-Fi	$10	$22
Zandar	$8	$22
Zarana w/earrings	$35	$125
Zarana w/o earrings	$10	$25
Lifeline	$10	$29
Low-Light	$8	$22
Dial-Tone	$8	$22
Leatherneck	$10	$25
Wet-Suit	$10	$29
Roadblock 2	$10	$25
Mainframe	$8	$22
Hawk 2	$8	$22
BAT Battle Android Trooper	$10	$25
Cobra Viper Trooper	$10	$25
Dr. Mindbender	$8	$22
Dreadnok Monkeywrench	$8	$22
Conquest X-30 Plane	$25	$75
Slipstream Figure from Conquest	$8	N/A

Tomahawk Helicopter	$25	$88
Lift Ticket from Tomahawk	$8	N/A
Triple T Tank	$22	$45
Sgt. Slaughter from Triple T Tank	$8	N/A
Devil Fish	$6	$15
LCV Recon Sled	$4	$10
Cobra Night Raven Jet	$18	$65
Strato Viper Pilot from Raven	$8	N/A
Cobra STUN	$15	$35
Motor Viper from STUN	$8	N/A
Dreadnok Thunder Machine	$17	$45
Thrasher Driver from Thunder Machine	$9	N/A
Serpentor with Air Chariot	$16	$50
Serpentor from above	$12	N/A

Sci-Fi says "I dare you to call me a geek!" $8-$10. *Courtesy of Play With This.*

Heavy Metal, driver of the Mauler MBT tank. Notice his often-lost microphne is lost, as it often is. As is, $10-$12. *Courtesy of Play With This.*

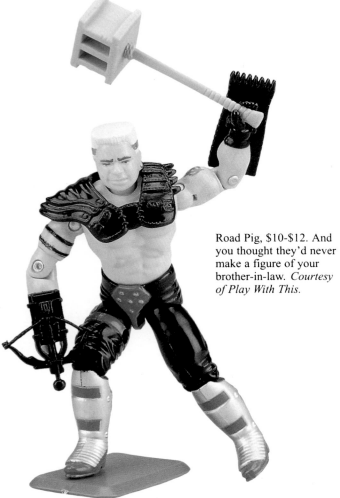

Road Pig, $10-$12. And you thought they'd never make a figure of your brother-in-law. *Courtesy of Play With This.*

Dreadnok Swampfire	$6	$15
Hydro Sled	$5	$15
Cobra Battle Gear Accessory Pack	$5	$15
Outpost Defender	$3	$10
L.A.W.	$3	$8
Cobra Surveillance Port	$3	$11
1987		
Crazylegs	$6	$16
Gung Ho Dress Outfit	$6	$16
Croc Master	$12	$30
Techno-Viper	$6	$15
Raptor	$9	$25
Fast Draw	$6	$16
Sneek Peek	$6	$15
Chuckles	$10	$18
Tunnel Rat	$12	$29
Jinx	$12	$29
Cobra Commander in Armor	$12	$29
Crystal Ball	$6	$15
Big Boa	$11	$26
Outback	$7	$18
Psyche-Out	$7	$18
Law & Order	$10	$25
Fridge Mail-In	$25	$35
Sgt. Slaughter Mail-In	$22	$28
Persuader	$21	$42
Backstop figure from Persuader	$11	N/A
HAVOC	$25	$55
Cross-Country figure from HAVOC	$10	N/A
Crossfire R/C Vehicle	$65	$155
Rumbler from Crossfire	$31	N/A
Coastal Defender	$4	$10
Road Toad	$4	$10
Cobra Mamba Helicopter	$12	$25
Gyro-Viper from Mamba	$6	N/A
Cobra Maggot	$21	$50

Listen up, maggot! Sergeant Slaughter has joined the Joes, but make sure he has his little stick before shelling out $12-$15 for him. *Courtesy of Play With This.*

The Dreadnoks: Torch, Ripper, and Buzzer, each $10-$12. Torch is slighlty higher at $12-$15. (his breath is better). *Courtesy of Play With This.*

Zartan, leader of the Dreadnoks, mint in box with Swamp Skier. Combining a figure with a mini-vehicle proved to be a good way to squeeze an extra 2 or 3 bucks out of kids. $100-$125. *Courtesy of Play With This.*

WORMS Maggot Driver	$15	N/A	Cobra Jet Pack	$3	$12
Cobra Sea Ray	$17	$39	Cobra Buzz Boar	$3	$7
Sea Slug Pilot from Sea Ray	$9	N/A	Windup Motorized Battle Packs (8)	$3	$7
Cobra Wolf ice vehicle	$17	$42	Defiant Space Shuttle complex	$175	$350
Ice-Viper from Wolf	$9	N/A	Hard Top Complex Driver	$25	N/A
Dreadnok Pirate Zanzibar w/Air Skiff	$9	$22	Payload Shuttle Pilot	$25	N/A
Zanzibar from above	$6	N/A	Mobile Command Center	$39	$125
Sgt. Slaughter's Renegades 3-Pack	$30	$60	Steam Roller, Center Driver	$22	N/A
Cobra-La Team Three-Pack	$35	$65	**1988**		
Dreadnok Cycle	$6	$15	Blizzard	$6	$15
Pogo Battle Ball	$4	$11	Storm Shadow 2	$12	$25

Repeater	$6	$12
Shockwave	$6	$12
Hit & Run	$12	$22
Iron Grenadier	$6	$12
Voltar	$8	$18
Road Pig	$12	$26
Lightfoot	$6	$15
Hardball	$6	$15
Spearhead	$6	$18
Muskrat	$6	$18
Charbroil	$6	$15
Toxo-Viper	$6	$15
Astro-Viper	$6	$15
Hydro-Viper	$6	$18
Budo	$5	$14
Dodger (BF 2000)	$6	$25
Maverick (BF 2000)	$6	$25
Blocker (BF 2000)	$6	$25
Blocker w/clear visor	$6	$25
Avalanche (BF2000)	$6	$25
Blaster (BF 2000)	$6	$25
Knockdown (BF 2000)	$6	$25
Tele-Viper (Python Patrol)	$5	$12
Viper (Python Patrol)	$5	$12
Copperhead (Python Patrol)	$5	$12
Cobra Officer (Python Patrol)	$5	$12
Crimson Guard (Python Patrol)	$5	$12
Cobra Trooper (Python Patrol)	$5	$12
Eliminator (BF 2000)	$6	$20
Vindicator (BF 2000)	$6	$20
Vector Jet (BF 2000)	$6	$20
Sky Sweeper (BF 2000)	$6	$20
Marauder (BF 2000)	$6	$20
Dominator (BF 2000)	$6	$20
Thunder (BF 2000)	$6	$20
Rolling Thunder	$50	$125
Armadillo Thunder Driver	$18	N/A
Phantom X-19 Stealth Plane	$41	$95
Stealth Pilot	$16	N/A
Mean Dog	$25	$60
Wild Card from Mean Dog	$15	N/A
Warthog A.I.F.V.	$14	$48
Sgt. Slaughter from Warthog	$8	N/A
Skystorm X-Wing Chopper	$12	$40
Windmill Pilot from Skystorm	$8	N/A
Desert Fox (6 wheel drive)	$21	$60

Up until then it was easy, but from that point it got real hard. Cobra hired evil twin brothers, leaders of the Crimson Guard. Pair $20-$24. *Courtesy of Play With This.*

Battlefield Forward Observer, one of the underappreciated accessory sets, $10-$12. *Courtesy of Play With This.*

Cobra FANG, it's the thang. $14-$16. *Courtesy of Play With This.*

Monkeywrench ($6-$8) asks Thrasher ($7-$9), "Ay, Dingo! 'Ow'd my 'ead get so bloomin' small?" Someone poured Alum in the Fosters, no doubt. *Courtesy of Play With This.*

Skidmark, Fox Driver	$11	N/A		Python Patrol ASP	$6	$12
R.P.V.	$4	$11		Python Patrol Conquest X-30	$15	$35
Swampmaster	$5	$13		**1989**		
Motorized mini-vehicles, each	$3	$8		Downtown	$5	$12
Cobra BUGG	$60	$125		Annihilator	$5	$14
Secto Viper, Bugg Driver	$18	N/A		Frag-Viper	$5	$12
Cobra Stellar Stiletto	$12	$22		Night-Viper	$5	$12
Star Viper Stiletto Pilot	$7	N/A		Deep Six	$5	$12
Cobra Battle Barge	$5	$12		Backblast	$5	$12
Cobra Adder	$3	$12		Stalker 2	$5	$15
Cobra Imp	$3	$12		HEAT Viper	$5	$15
Destro's Despoiler	$12	$35		Gnawgahyde	$5	$15
Destro from Despoiler	$8	N/A		Dee-Jay (BF 2000 '89)	$5	$12
AGP Anti-Gravity Pod	$12	$25		Rock 'N Roll #2	$5	$12
Nullifier AGP Pilot	$7	N/A		T.A.R.G.A.T.	$5	$12
Destro's D.E.M.O.N.	$14	$55		Recoil	$5	$12
Ferret, D.E.M.O.N. Pilot	$9	N/A		Snake Eyes	$10	$25
Python Patrol STUN	$6	$12		Countdown	$5	$12

A Tiger Force reissue of Cobra's Ferret
vehicle, here called Tiger Paw (Aww, Maw!).
$12-$15. *Courtesy of Play With This.*

Cobra FANG 2. You're welcome!
$12-$14. *Courtesy of Play With This.*

Sgt. Slaughter and his Triple T Tank, you know who you've
got to thank! $20-$22. *Courtesy of Play With This.*

Topside tops out at $20-$22 carded.
Courtesy of Play With This.

Chuckles, the undercover agent in a loud Hawaiian shirt.
Yeah, okay. $15-$18 carded. *Courtesy of Play With This.*

From Battleforce 2000 comes Avalanche. No thanks
I just 'ad one. $20-$25. *Courtesy of Play With This.*

B.F. 2000's Blaster puts a hole in your savings to
the tune of $20-$25. *Courtesy of Play With This.*

Scoop	$5	$12
Alley Viper	$7	$18
Duke (Tiger Force)	$8	$22
Roadblock (Tiger Force)	$8	$22
Flint (Tiger Force)	$8	$22
Bazooka (Tiger Force)	$8	$22
Tripwire (Tiger Force)	$8	$22
Dusty (Tiger Force)	$8	$22
Lifeline (Tiger Force)	$8	$22
Psyche-Out (T.F. Europe Only)	$15	$35
Outback (T.F. Europe Only)	$15	$35
Tunnel Rat (T.F. Europe Only)	$15	$35
Hit & Run (T.F. Europe Only)	$15	$35
Sneak Peek T.F. (Europe Only)	$15	$35
Blizzard (T.F. Europe Only)	$15	$35
Sgt. Slaughter (Marauders)	$8	$19
Footloose (Marauders)	$6	$14
Low-Light (Marauders)	$6	$14
Spirit (Marauders)	$6	$13
Barbecue (Marauders)	$6	$13
Mutt & Junkyard (Marauders)	$9	$22
Airborne (Sky Patrol)	$11	$28
Airwave (Sky Patrol)	$11	$28
Altitude (Sky Patrol)	$11	$28
Drop Zone (Sky Patrol)	$11	$28
Skydive (Sky Patrol)	$11	$28
Static Line (Sky Patrol)	$11	$28
Falcon/Sneek Peek (Night Force)	$24	$49
Tunnel-Rat/Psyche-Out (Night Force)	$24	$49
Outback /Crazylegs (Night Force)	$24	$49
Cobra Condor	$21	$55

BF 2000's Maverick garners about $20-$25 carded. *Courtesy of Play With This.*

The Cobra Battle Barge barges into your heart for a mere $10-$12. *Courtesy of Play With This.*

One of the least popular accessories, the Cobra Jet Pack flies home with you for $10-$12 boxed. *Courtesy of Play With This.*

Aero-Viper Condor Pilot	$11	N/A
Cobra HISS 2	$19	$48
Track Viper HISS 2 Driver	$11	N/A
Darklon w/Evader	$12	$27
Darklon from above	$8	N/A
Razorback	$18	$48
Wild Boar, Razorback driver	$9	N/A
Thunderclap Long Range Cannon	$66	$104
Long Range, Thuderclap Driver	$16	N/A
Raider	$30	$66
Hotseat, Raider Driver	$8	N/A
Arctic Blast	$15	$35
Windchill, Blast Driver	$8	N/A
Mudfighter vehicle	$15	$35
Dogfight, driver from Mudfighter	$7	N/A
Crusader Space Shuttle	$35	$75
Payload, Shuttle Pilot	$15	N/A
HISS 2/Mudfighter Two-Pack	$95	$175
Tiger Force Vehicles		
Tiger Rat	$30	$96
Skystriker (Tiger Rat Pilot)	$12	N/A
Tiger Fly (Tiger Force Dragonfly)	$26	$75
Recondo (Fly Pilot)	$12	N/A

Tiger Cat (Tiger Force Snowcat)	$18	$65
Frostbite (Tiger Cat Driver)	$10	N/A
Tiger Paw	$6	$15
Tiger Shark	$6	$15
Tiger Fish	$6	$15
Tiger Sting	$6	$15
Night Force Vehicles		
Night Shade	$25	$50
Night Blaster	$15	$27
Night Raider	$15	$27
Night Storm	$15	$27
Night Striker	$25	$50
Night Scrambler	$25	$50
Night Ray	$25	$50
Night Boomer	$29	$60
Sky (Patrol) Hawk	$15	$32
Sky SHARC	$15	$32
Sky HAVOC	$16	$38
Sky Raven	$27	$55
Slaughter's Marauders Vehicles		
Equalizer	$6	$12
Armadillo Mini Tank (Marauders)	$6	$12
Lynx	$6	$12

This Asian reissue of Major Bludd can be had for a mere $12-$14, what the original goes for loose. *Courtesy of Play With This.*

Tiger Force Roadblock says "We'll end this chapter with a blast! Because they saved the best for last!" Excelsior! $12-$14 on Asian card. *Courtesy of Play With This.*

"What the heck is this chapter all about?" you may rightly ask.

This is the chapter that focuses on action-adventure characters popularized through cartoon series which were intended to promote a toy line. Known as "half hour commercials," they acted as advertisements not only for the figures themselves, but their vehicles and accessories as well, all of which were shown and demonstrated in action. The figures which were "advertised" in many of the half-hour commercials can be found in other chapters in this book. Ones which are based on movies and use the character's likeness (like Rambo) are in Chapter 9, Movie and TV Characters. Ones that are heavily based in fantasy worlds (like ThunderCats) are in the fantasy chapter. The big names like G.I.Joe and He-Man have chapters of their own. This chapter, basically, is where I put everybody else.

BIONIC SIX evokes many happy memories of getting ready for morning classes at Brooklyn High School grades 13-16, otherwise known as Brooklyn College, to which I transferred after two years at Sarah Lawrence, for reasons I still can't recall. This series is known for its catchy theme song and figures made of die-cast metal instead of plastic.

BRAVESTARR was a space western set on a planet that resembled a frontier town, where the residents were aliens who acted in traditional cowboy movie ways. Conflicts arose whenever evil Tex Hex and his band of owlhoots would try to rustle up some precious Kerium. The figures were a stocky 8" tall and featured interactive laser weaponry. There was also a kid-sized gun that worked with the figures.

CAPTAIN POWER is from the same era. It seems that everybody got on the half hour commercial bandwagon at the same time, because a huge wave of them crashed into our homes in 1986. Captain Power was an unusual LIVE-ACTION half-hour commercial, as opposed to being a cartoon. The show plugged a series of action figures which had interactive weapons that could fire at the TV and actually register hits during the Captain Power program. There was also a video tape available, if you didn't get the show in your area. My Micronaut buddy Steve Ross has always thought of Captain Power as a kind of Micronauts: The Next Generation, but unfortunately the line didn't catch on. Among the short-lived lines of the 1980s, this is one of the most sought-after today.

CENTURIONS is a sadly-overlooked line of seven-inch characters whose modular costumes allowed them to be plugged into assorted weapons systems. The systems were also interchangeable, allowing for all sorts of cool combinations. This line combined G.I.Joe-style

Bionic Six'
F.L.U.F.F.I. ($4-$5)
and Klunk ($3-$4).
*Courtesy of J.E.
Alvarez.*

Marshal Bravestarr and Tex Hex two-pack,
$20-$25. *Courtesy of Play With This.*

Handlebar, with
plate-throwing
action (plates
not shown),
complete $4-$6.
*Courtesy of Play
With This.*

characters with Micronauts-style play value. It didn't click, perhaps because of the size, which made it incompatible with other toy lines, just like the less-interesting Bravestarr line.

There isn't much to say about CHUCK NORRIS KARATE COMMANDOS. The figures were a respectable 6" size and had cool action features. I could never figure out why it didn't take off. It blows away its closest competition, the Karate Kid series.

COPS has always been a pet love of mine. I had always wished that Hasbro had made their 1980s G.I.Joe a tad bigger—say six inches, while retaining the super articulation that made the concept so popular. Well, COPS was exactly that. The figures were awesome, but the line was done in by an overly-campy, babyish half-hour commercial and comic book. I spent most of 1990 (and most of my income IN 1990) gathering up all the COPS figures I could at closeout prices, much to my girlfriend's understandable consternation. But this line has yet to become the sleeper hit I thought it would be. Eventually, during one of my frequent flat-broke periods, I sold them all off, and not for a profit, either. Part of the problem with COPS never catching on with collectors is that the coolest figures of all were in the never-released third series. I've seen photos, and this last line really captured that spirit of zany destruction that gave the toy line its flavor. Toy expert Thomas Wheeler once told me that what few prototypes and production samples there were had been GROUND UP by Hasbro! A sad end to what I personally believe to be THE BEST action figure line of the 1980s.

EAGLE FORCE was a line of die cast metal action figures created by Mego as a kind of mini-war scenario. (The figures were only two inches tall.) Nobody cared.

The mid-80s also saw a war between rival "Ghostbusters." The theatrical film had us in spasms over ectoplasms, and of course Kenner got the license. But Filmation was able to mount a heavily-promoted "me too" line and a cartoon to go with it. How? Well, in the 1970s there had been ANOTHER Ghostbusters. This one was a live-action, half hour Saturday morning TV show that reunited Forrest Tucker and Larry Storch and featured Tracy the Gorilla, designed and played by Bob Burns. Anyway, Filmation's cartoon was loosely based on the Tucker/Storch show. This animated version was an incredibly unbearable pile of ghost manure, de-composed of characters with the most infantile names and speech patterns I've ever had the displeasure of accidentally seeing three seconds of. True to form, the action figure line was its toy equivalent.

Meanwhile, the "real" Ghostbusters TV cartoon and toy line, which were ACTUALLY CALLED *The Real Ghostbusters* to show up the competition, were going great guns. The carefully-chosen title allowed the producers to repeatedly jab at the competition. "The REAL Ghostbusters will be back after these messages," and so on. The line itself incorporated every action feature in the book, enabling kids to act out the same kinds of hilarious and exciting adventures that the outstanding cartoon presented on weekdays and Saturdays. (The cartoon was, in fact, far superior to the movies.)

INHUMANOIDS looked like a winner. A group of scientists battle gigantic underground invaders, assisted by friendly(er) underground creatures. But the sense of scale was off. The humans should have been about two inches tall, but they came wearing non-removable exoskeletons which made them larger and more capable of doing battle with the monsters. This translated in reality into 7" figures with the heads of 2" figures under their easily-lost helmets. Result: No sales. But the monsters were huge, about fifteen inches tall, and are avidly sought by monster toy collectors. Ahh, what might have

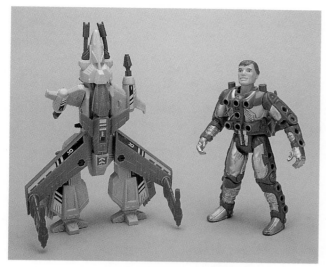

Centurions Ace McCloud ($4-$5) confronts one of
Dr. Terror's Strafer jet drones ($4-$6). Accessories
not shown. *Courtesy of Play With This.*

Chuck Norris works out.
$4-$5 as shown. *Courtesy
of Play With This.*

been ... I was at Brooklyn College that year and was
able to see the huge, Hollywoodish Inhumanoids cave
display that FAO Schwarz had in their Manhattan store
that Christmas.

Meanwhile, M.A.S.K. had everything going for it,
but only lasted a short time anyway. It attempted to combine G.I.Joe-like cool characters with vehicles that transformed. But the small size of the figures (which made
the whole thing economical enough to produce) put off
action figure fans. And transforming vehicle fans were
happy enough with their Transformers.

PHOTON was, like Captain Power, a live-action half
hour commercial. The only toy that made it to stores
was a two-pack of the main hero and a henchman villain, but the figures were about 10" tall and really cool
looking. Photon was based on the popular laser-light
war game and the playset incorporated those features,
not unlike the Bravestarr line.

Revell took one of their infrequent shots at action
figures with POWER LORDS, a group of futuristic
aliens, each with a special gimmick. The figures in this
series looked so damn WEIRD that people would pick
them up in the store, go "UGH!", and drop them again.
But they score high on the Neat-O Scale.

I have an anectdote about ROBOTECH. I was never
much for Japanese animation, which is what the half-
hour commercial for Robotech was composed of.
Robotech is part of a much-larger epic, and these
"anime" epics inspire great loyalty among the people
who like this stuff. Sometimes that loyalty transforms
into a kind of love. But, as the noted social satirist Barrie
Evans pointed out, when they kiss the TV screen they
get little pricklies on their lips. But I digress. Personally, I always thought the characters looked too distorted,
and found the animation far too repetitive. I used to call
the show "Robot Ecch."

Anyway ... when Robotech was on, I had two friends
who, in their college years, would get stoned off their
butts and debate the intricacies of the storyline. They
could never agree on what Protoculture, the Kerium of
the Robotech world, actually was. That's the anectdote.
Anyway, the REAL reason I don't like Japanese animation is that it supplanted, to a large degree, Japanese
LIVE-ACTION, and I am a huge Space Giants,
Ultraman, and Johnny Sokko fan.

SGT. ROCK was a Remco line that was intended as
a G.I.Joe knockoff. But it was also the first figure line
of the 1980s to be based on a DC comic book, the adventures of the inimitable Sergeant Frank Rock. The
highlights of the line are its environmental playsets that
feature machine gun nests and the like.

STARCOM was yet another misfired attempt by
Coleco to get a solid action figure line going. This in-
volved astronaut figures, two inches tall, like Mego's
Eagle Force, which didn't sell either. The package art-
work was gorgeous, though.

STEEL MONSTERS was a cool series of Mad Max-
type vehicles with drivers. It appealed more to the truck
crowd than the action figure crowd.

TEAM AMERICA was a short-lived series of 8"
action figures with limited posability, designed to ride
cycles and other vehicles. It featured a spin-off Marvel
comic that spotlighted Captain America, who they really, really should have included in the figure line.

And there's your rundown of the Real Men (and
women) of the half hour commercials of the 1980s.

Sgt. Mace, one of the top COPS, $18-$20.
Courtesy of Play With This.

Air Wave flies home at $12-$15.
Courtesy of Play With This.

This COP is also a firefighter. Inferno,
$10-$12. *Courtesy of Play With This.*

"We're gonna knock over the bank, see?" Big Boss
($5-$6) gives instructions to Koo-Koo ($5-$6).
Accessories not shown. *Courtesy of Play With This.*

The figure that got me into COPS, Dr. Badvibes, $15-$18 carded. *Courtesy of Play With This.*

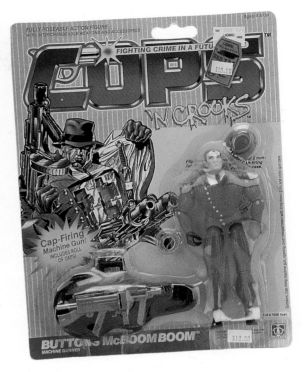

The figure that most fans like best, hoodlum Buttons Mc Boom Boom, with guns that pop out of his double-breasted suit. $15-$18 *Courtesy of Play With This.*

REAL MEN ACTION FIGURES

ITEM	LMC	MIP
BIONIC SIX (LJN 1986)		
J.D.	$3	$10
Meg	$3	$10
Eric	$3	$10
Bunji	$5	$20
Helen	$3	$10
Jack	$3	$10
FLUFFI	$5	$20
Dr.Scarab	$3	$10
Klunk	$3	$10
Glove	$3	$10
Chopper	$3	$10
Quad Runner	$5	$15
Dirt Bike	$5	$15
Laser Chair	$5	$15
Scarab's Laser Throne	$5	$15
MULES Van	$6	$20
Headquarters Playset	$9	$25
BRAVESTARR (Mattel 1986)		
Marshal Bravestarr	$6	$12
Tex Hex	$6	$12
Bravestarr/Tex Hex Two Pack	$12	$25
Handle Bar	$6	$12
Thunder Stick	$6	$12
Thirty/Thirty	$7	$14
Deputy Fuzz	$7	$14
Outlaw Scuzz	$7	$14
Skull Walker	$5	$10
Sand Storm	$5	$10
Laser Fire Marshall Bravestar	$7	$14
Laser Fire Tex Hex	$7	$14
Neutra-Laser	$6	$12
Laser Fire Backpack	$6	$12
Fort Kerium Playset	$12	$24
CAPTAIN POWER (Mattel 1987)		
Captain Power	$4	$10
Major Hawk Masterson	$4	$10
Lt. Tank Ellis	$4	$10

Carded Koo-Koo, with his clock-hands daggers and time bomb. This line was too cool to survive. $15-$18. *Courtesy of Play With This.*

Lord Dread	$4	$10
Soaron	$4	$10
Blastarr	$4	$10
Pilot Chase	$6	$18
Scout Baker	$6	$15
Stingray Johnson	$10	$25
Tritor	$12	$35
Dread Trooper (Not Released?)		
Dread Commander(Not Released?)		
Power On Energizer	$4	$10

Eagle Force figures from Mego, $2-$3 each. *Courtesy of Play With This.*

Ghostbusters Egon, $12-$14. *Courtesy of Play With This.*

Interlocker Throne	$4	$10
Magna Cycle	$70	$25
Dread Stalker	$5	$14
TransField Base Station	$5	$20
Communications Station	$5	$20
Phantom Striker	$8	$19
Power Base Fortress	$10	$25
Power Jet XT7	$8	$25
Power Jet XT7 with video	$10	$29

CENTURIONS (Kenner 1986)

Max Ray	$5	$10
Ace McCloud	$5	$10
Jake Rockwell	$5	$10
Dr.Terror	$7	$14
Hacker	$7	$14
Strafer Robot	$6	$12
Weapons Systems, each	$6	$12
Wild Weasel, Hornet, Detonator, Skybolt		
Orbital Interceptor, Tidal Blast, Depth Charger		
Figural Flashlights	$3	$6

CHUCK NORRIS KARATE COMMANDOS (Kenner 1986)

Chuck Norris (3 assorted versions)	$5	$15
Tabe	$3	$9
Kimo	$3	$9
Reed Smith	$3	$9
Ninja Warrior	$4	$16
Ninja Master	$4	$16
Ninja Serpent	$4	$16
SuperNinja	$4	$16
Karate Corvette	$6	$19

Ghostbusters Mummy, $10-$12 carded. *Courtesy of Play With This.*

COPS (Hasbro 1988)

Sgt. Mace	$6	$20
Officer Bowser and Blitz	$8	$22
Bullet-Proof	$8	$22
Longarm	$8	$22
Barricade	$4	$12
Highway	$5	$15
Sundown	$5	$15
Inferno	$4	$12
Airwave	$5	$15
Powder Keg (either packaging version)	$6	$18
Nightstick	$5	$15
Checkpoint	$6	$18
Taser	$5	$15

APES	$5	$15
Crooks		
Big Boss	$6	$18
Buttons McBoom Boom	$6	$18
Berserko	$5	$15
Dr.Badvibes w/Robot	$5	$15
Rock Krusher	$5	$15
Louie The Plumber	$6	$18
Hyena	$5	$15
Bullitt	$7	$20
Koo Koo	$6	$18
Nightmare	$4	$12
Vehicles		
Air Speeder	$3	$9

Ghostbusters Werewolf, $10-$12.
Courtesy of Play With This.

Pursuit Jet	$3	$10
Roadster w/Turbo Tutone	$12	$25
Highway Interceptor w/Road Block	$12	$25
ATAC w.Heavyweight	$10	$22
Assault Vehicle w/Hard Top	$10	$20
Evil Ventriloquist (Not Released)		
State Trooper (Not Released)		
Air-Assault Cop (Not Released)		
Android Cop (Not Released)		
Sewer Rat Crook (Not Released)		
Tongue-Action Prankster Clown (Not Released)		
Water-Squirting Prankster Clown (Not Released)		

EAGLE FORCE (Mego 1981)

Figures, each	$2	$5
Eliminator Jeep	$4	$10
Talon Tank	$4	$10
Communications Set w/figure	$4	$10
Eagle Island Playset	$9	$18

FILMATION'S GHOSTBUSTERS (Schaper 1986)

Eddie	$5	$10
Jake	$5	$10
Tracy	$5	$10
Fangster	$5	$10
Fib Face	$5	$10
Haunter	$5	$10
Mysteria	$5	$10
Prime Evil	$5	$10
Scared Stiff	$5	$10
Jessica	$5	$10
Belfry	$5	$10
Futura	$5	$10
Bone Troller	$7	$15
Scare Scooter	$6	$13
Time Hopper	$8	$20
Ghost Buggy	$8	$25

Ghostbusters Dracula, $10-$12.
Courtesy of Play With This.

Ghostbusters Zombie, $10-$12.
Courtesy of Play With This.

Ecto-1 car, $40-$50 boxed. *Courtesy of Play With This.*

Ghostbusters Hunchback, not a real modo but a quasi modo (with apologies to Forry Ackerman). $10-$12. *Courtesy of Play With This.*

THE (REAL) GHOSTBUSTERS (Kenner 1988)

Egon w/Gulper	$14	$30
Peter W/Grabber	$15	$30
Ray w/Wrapper	$15	$30
Winston w/Chomper	$15	$30
Slimer w/food pieces	$18	$40
Sta-Puft Marshmallow Man	$19	$45
Bug Eye/H2O/Bad Bone Ghosts	$15	$30
Gooper Ghosts, each	$5	$15
Banshee/Squisher		
Ecto-1	$29	$69
Fire House	$20	$50
Fright Features Heroes, each	$4	$15
Gooper Ghost Slimer	$10	$25
Fright Feature Ghosts, each	$4	$12
Granny/Hard Hat/Mail Fraud/		
Terror Trash/Tombstine Tackle/X-Cop	$4	$12
Mini-Ghosts: Gooper/Trap/Shooter ea.	$3	$9
Pull Speed Ahead	$3	$9
Brain Blaster	$3	$9
Highway Haunter	$3	$9
Ghost Spooker	$3	$9
Ecto-2	$5	$15
Screamin' Heroes, each	$5	$15
Super Fright Feature Heroes, each	$5	$15
Slimer w/proton pack	$10	$35
Universal-style Monsters, each	$4	$12
Fearsome Flush Toilet Monster	$2	$9

Leader of the Inhumanoids' rock men, whose shell is a separate figure, $3-$4. *Courtesy of J.E. Alvarez.*

Inhumanoid rock men, $2-$3. *Courtesy of J.E. Alvarez.*

M.A.S.K. figures, $3-$4 each. *Courtesy of Play With This.*

Robotech's Scott Bernard, $30-$35 carded. *Courtesy of Play With This.*

Ecto-3	$4	$10
Ecto-500	$4	$10
Power Pack Heroes, each	$5	$15
Slimed Heroes, each	$4	$12
Gobblin Goblins, each	$5	$16
Ghost Sweeper	$4	$9
Ecto 1-A	$18	$50
Ecto-Bomber	$4	$12
Ecto Blaster	$4	$12
Ecto-Glow Heroes, each	$12	$30
Backpack Heroes (Not Released)		

INHUMANOIDS (Hasbro 1986)

Dr. Derek Bright	$3	$5
Herc Armstrong	$3	$5
Liquidator	$3	$5
Auger	$3	$5
Granites, 2 versions, each	$3	$7
Magnokor the 2-in-1 Granite	$4	$9
Redwoods, 2 versions, each	$3	$7
Terrascout Vehicle	$3	$7
Trappeur Vehicle	$3	$7
Metlar Inhumanoid Leader	$25	$55
Tendril Inhumanoid Plant Beast	$30	$60
D'Compose Inhumanoid Skelton	$30	$60

M.A.S.K. (Kenner 1985)
Figure Two-packs

Matt Tracker and Miles Mayhem,	$5	$12
Matt Tracker and Hondo MacLean	$4	$10
Bruce Sato and Brad Turner	$4	$10
Cliff Dagger and Sly Rax	$4	$10
Alex Sector and Buddie Hawks	$5	$10
T-Bob and Scott Trakker	$4	$10
Adventure Packs, each	$3	$9
Jungle Challenge, Rescue Mission, Coast Patrol, Venom's Revenge		
Alex Sector and Buddie Hawks	$5	$10
Thunderhawk w/figure	$3	$9
Condor w/figure	$3	$9
Piranha w/figure	$3	$9
Gator w/figure	$3	$9
Jackhammer w/figure	$3	$9
Switchblade w/figure	$3	$9
Rhino w/ figures	$6	$12

Robotech's Miriya, $20-$25 for the "red" version carded. *Courtesy of Play With This.*

Zentraedi Warrior $15-$18 carded.
Courtesy of Play With This.

Robetech's Rand carded, $7-$9.
Courtesy of Play With This.

Corg carded can come home for $10-$12.
Courtesy of Play With This.

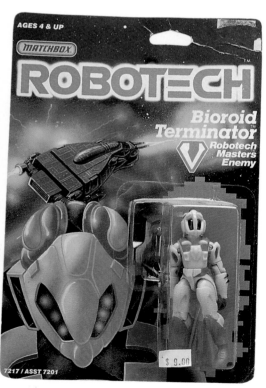

Bioroid Terminator terminates $15-$18 of
your money. *Courtesy of Play With This.*

Vampire w/figure	$3	$9
Firefly w/figure	$3	$9
Raven w/figure	$3	$9
Firecracker w/figure	$3	$9
Stinger w/figure	$4	$9
Hurricane w/figure	$3	$9
Slingshot w/figure	$3	$9
Volcano w/figures	$5	$15
Outlaw w/figures	$5	$15
"Split Seconds" Skybolt Vehicle	$7	$18
"The Collector" Playset w/figure	$3	$9
Boulder Hill Playset w/figures	$12	$28

PHOTON (LJN 1986)

Bhodi-Lee vs Warrior Set	$20	$35

POWER LORDS (Revell 1982)

Figures, each	$6	$20
Adam Power, Arkus, Bakatak, Disguyzor Drrench, Ggriptogg, Raygoth, Shaya, Sydot, Tork		
Trigore Vehicle w/figure	$12	$28
Volcan Rock Headquarters	$18	$35

ROBOTECH (Matchbox 1986)

Rick Hunter	$5	$20
Dana Sterling	$10	$28
Lynn Minimei	$50	$150
Corg	$3	$12
Lunk	$8	$12
Max Sterling	$8	$15
Rand	$3	$9
Robotech Master	$3	$9
Rook Bartley	$10	$55
Roy Fokker	$3	$19
Scott Bernard	$4	$35
Zor Prime	$3	$8
Micronized Zentradi	$3	$9
Bioroid Terminator	$6	$18
Miriya(Red)	$5	$25
Miriya(Black)	$20	$75

Miriya (Purple)	$50	$150
Miriya 6" Figure	$4	$20
Breeti	$3	$15
Dolza	$4	$15
Exedore	$4	$15
Khyron	$4	$15
Armored Zentradi	$4	$15
Battloids, each	$6	$28
Small Accessories, each	$9	$35
Mid-sized accessories, each	$15	$50
6" Scott Bernard w/Armored Cyclone	$15	$50
SDF-1 Playset	$50	$140
12" Figures		
Rick Hunter	$15	$45
Lisa Hayes	$10	$30
Lynn Minmei	$10	$15
Dana Sterling	$10	$30
Dana's Hover Cycle	$10	$25
Minmei's Fanliner (Not Released)		
Outfits, each	$5	$12

SGT. ROCK (Remco 1982)

Sgt. Rock	$10	$50
Other Figures	$3	$10
Vehicles, each	$10	$25
Playsets, each	$12	$30

STARCOM (Coleco 1986)

Figures, each	$1	$3
Mid-Sized Vehicles, each	$5	$8
Large Vehicles, each	$8	$15
Starbase Station	$10	$20

STEEL MONSTERS (Tonka 1986)

Carded Figures, each	$2	$4
Vehicles w/figures, each	$5	$12

TEAM AMERICA (Ideal 1982)

Figures, each	$2	$4
Engergizer	$2	$4
Vehicles, each	$3	$6

The Sarge is a rock-solid investment at $40-$50, but the villains and other figures, at about ten bucks apiece, melt like ice cream soldiers. *Courtesy of Steven Silvia.*

HE-MAN AND THE MASTERS OF THE UNIVERSE

He-Man came out of nowhere.

Imagine that you are in a toy store on a warm summer day in 1982. You expect to see a lot of Star Wars and G.I.Joe figures—all the same size, roughly the same build. Of course, the G.I.Joe figures are three times as posable as the Star Wars figures, but I digress.

Suddenly you see a much larger, much chunkier figure hanging nearby. You take a look at it—it's some kind of fantasy warrior. Look at those cool accessories! Look at that weird squatting position! Boy, this is great!

That was my personal first encounter with He-Man, and I bet a lot of other people had a similar experience. Mattel succeeded in introducing an entirely new action figure product category—the bulky, squatting warrior figure. They did it by combining a thriftily-assembled figure line (which often recycled arms and legs on different characters) and an insipid but popular cartoon show to produce some magnificent marketing muscle. The result was a steady half-decade of sales and a scad of imitators. Mattel had finally given the world a boys' toy to rival the success of their Barbie—at least, for a while.

As the years rolled on, the brains at Mattel thought up stranger and stranger characters, and found wilder and wilder ways to reuse old arms, legs—even whole figures. He-Man was available repainted as Faker, a robot duplicate. Beast-Man was covered with green flocking to become Moss-Man. Mer-Man had a complete makeover as the evil skunk Stinkor. Names got sillier too, with my all-time favorite being Clawful. "My, that's a claw full!"

Just after his fifth anniversary, He-Man suffered a sales decline. Although the live-action Masters of The Universe movie, pitting Dolph Lundgren against Frank Langella, was entertaining, it did nothing for sales of the line.

But He-Man wasn't gone for long. In 1989, the line was completely revamped with non-squatting action figures. Now, the emphasis was more toward straight sci-fi. However, it didn't catch on, because it lacked the lovable corniness and the air of comfortable cheapness that made the earlier series so appealingly appalling. Not far into the new decade, The Masters of the Universe went to that great Metamucil factory in the sky.

Beast Man! Not your ex-husband, but a remarkable reconstruction,. $25-$28. *Courtesy of Play With This.*

Not Cyclops or Biclops but Tri-Klops, $20-$25 carded. *Courtesy of Play With This.*

Stratos, a first series figure, $25-$30 carded. *Courtesy of Play With This.*

The back of Stratos' card shows the first series figures.

Sorceress spreads her wings, $12-$15. *Courtesy of Play With This.*

Teela, without armor so you can see her exquisite detailing. As is, $8-$10. *Courtesy of Play With This.*

Left:
Man-E-Faces, the
ultimate agent. $20-
$25 carded.
*Courtesy of Play
With This.*

Below:
Immortalized in the
Bo Diddley line, "Bo
Diddley called up
Battle Cat," here he
is, $26-$30 boxed.
*Courtesy of Play
With This.*

I'd make a joke that Faker should have
been a female figure, but I don't need
that kind of e-mail. $22-$25 carded.
Courtesy of Play With This.

HE-MAN AND THE MASTERS OF THE UNIVERSE

(Mattel 1982)

ITEM	LMC	MIP
He-Man	$10	$35
Man-At-Arms	$10	$30
Stratos	$10	$30
Zodac	$12	$30
Teela	$15	$35
Skeletor	$13	$38
Beast-Man	$12	$28
Mer-Man	$14	$30
Faker	$12	$30
Battle Cat	$10	$30
Wind Raider	$8	$25
Battle Ram	$8	$25
Castle Grayskull	$30	$85
1983 Series		
Ram Man	$8	$25
Mekanek	$7	$18
Man-E-Faces	$8	$25
Trap-Jaw	$9	$25
Tri-Klops	$9	$25

ITEM	LMC	MIP
Evil-Lyn	$12	$38
Panthor	$10	$25
Zoar	$8	$20
Screech	$8	$20
Attak Trak	$8	$18
Road Ripper	$8	$15
Point Dread w/Talon Fighter	$18	$40
1984 Series		
Battle Armor He-Man	$12	$28
Battle Armor Skeletor	$12	$28
Prince Adam	$10	$30
Buzz-Off	$8	$18
Fisto	$7	$20
Orko	$8	$25
Whiplash	$6	$20
Jitsu	$8	$22
Clawful	$10	$25
Webstor	$8	$20

Atak Trak got back. Dayum! $15-$18.
Courtesy of Play With This.

Two-Bad settles an argument his/their usual way. $4-$6 as shown. This was the second shot on the twenty-second roll of film used for this book, and was labelled 22/2. No I am not kidding. *Courtesy of Play With This.*

My favorite Masters character, Clawful. "My, that's a claw full!" $20-$25 carded. *Courtesy of Play With This.*

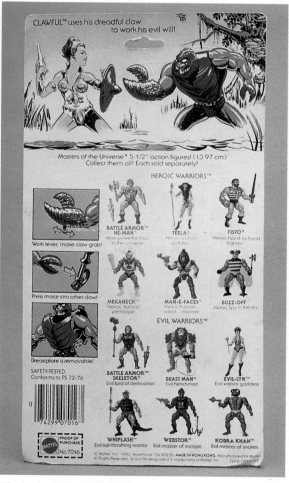

The back of Clawful's package shows the characters in that series.

Kobra Khan	$6	$18		Hordak	$6	$18
Roton	$5	$15		Leech	$6	$18
Stridor	$6	$20		Mantenna	$6	$18
Stridor w/Fisto	$15	$30		Grizzlor	$6	$18
Weapon Pack	$6	$15		Modulok	$8	$20
Dragon Walker	$4	$15		Bashasaurus	$10	$20
Snake Mountain	$40	$80		Land Shark	$8	$19
1985 Series				Spydor	$8	$25
Thunder Punch He-Man	$13	$26		Night Stalker	$6	$18
Dragon Blaster Skeletor	$13	$26		Battle Bones Carry Case	$5	$15
Roboto (Domo Arigato!)	$5	$15		Fright Zone	$15	$45
Sy-Klone	$5	$15		**1986 Series**		
Stonedar	$5	$12		Flying Fists He-Man	$12	$35
Rokkon	$5	$12		Terror Claws Skeletor	$15	$45
Moss Man	$5	$15		Hurricane Hordak	$13	$26
Stinkor	$6	$18		Snout Spout	$5	$15
Two-Bad	$6	$18		Rio Blast	$5	$15
Spikor	$6	$18		Extendar	$5	$15

Whiplash carded $18-$20.
Courtesy of Play With This.

Spikor, your one-stop shop
for all spy devices. $16-$18.
Courtesy of Play With This.

Orko in the package, sealed in, with
no air. Cross your fingers. $20-$25.
Courtesy of Play with This.

"He-Man, you've got to
make me more irritating,"
sez Orko, who begat
Gwildor, The Trobbits and
(shudder) Snarf. $6-$8 as
shown. *Courtesy of Play
With This.*

Sy-Klone spins into your heart for $12-$15. *Courtesy of Play With This.*

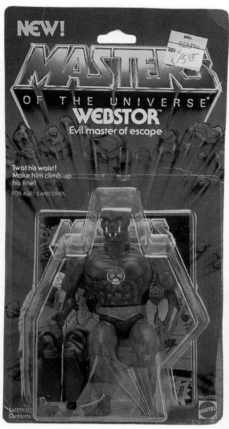

Webstor, the Emmanuel Lewis action figure. I've waited twelve years to make that joke. Yet now, somehow, I feel empty. $18-$20. *Courtesy of Play With This.*

Roton, the horrific vehicle. $12-$15 boxed. *Courtesy of Play With This.*

Moss Man, who is really Beast Man with green flocking. You explain it to me. $12-$15. *Courtesy of Play With This.*

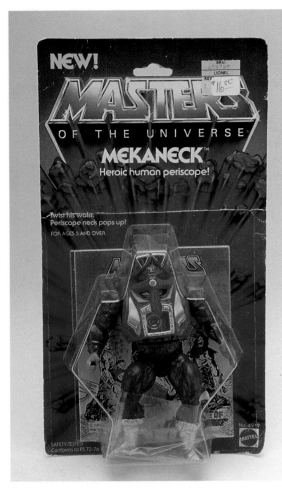

Mekanek charges himself a fortune. "That Pittman Arm's gotta be totally overhauled." $15-$18. *Courtesy of Play With This.*

I always liked Fisto. The Fisto/Strido two-pack came out first, and I almost bought it just for Fisto. Glad I waited for them to release him on his own. $18-$20. *Courtesy of Play With This.*

"Skeletor's got this creep, Spydor—He's got Master Power, puh puh puh puh POW!" Remember that commercial? No? Your loss. $20-$25. *Courtesy of Play With This.*

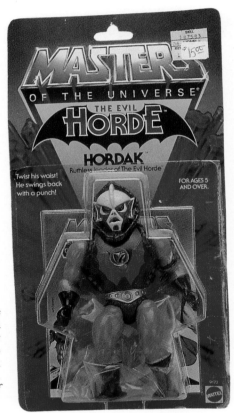

Hordak, leader of the Evil Horde. I've got a great Hordak story but you'll have to catch me at a book signing to hear it. $16-$18. *Courtesy of Play With This.*

Mantenna (hyulk) from the Evil Horde. Remember the commerical? "Leech! Mantenna! Grizzlor! Cro-o-owww!" $4-$6 as is. *Courtesy of Play With This.*

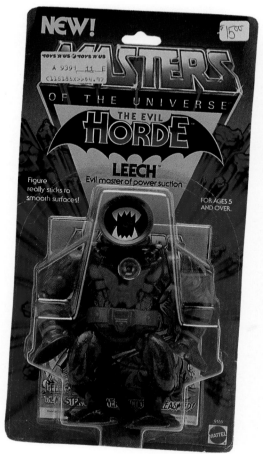

At last, an action figure of a toy dealer. Leech, $15-$18. *Courtesy of—and with all due respect to—Play With This.*

The back of Leech's package shows Grizzlor and Modulok and the Fright Zone playset. *Courtesy of Play With This.*

They made a playset out of your in-laws' rec rom! The Slime Pit, $20-$25 boxed. *Courtesy of Play With This.*

Dragstor	$5	$15
Horde Trooper	$5	$15
King Hiss	$5	$15
Tung Lashor	$5	$15
Multi-Bot	$6	$18
Gwildor (Movie Figure)	$10	$29
Saurod (Movie Figure)	$10	$29
Blade (Movie Figure)	$10	$29
Mantisaur	$6	$19
Monstroid	$6	$19
Blaster Hawk	$6	$18
Fright Fighter	$6	$18
Laser Bolt	$5	$15
Stilt Stalkers	$5	$15
Megalaser	$5	$15
Beam Blaster and Artilleray	$8	$22
Jet Sled	$5	$15
Slime Pit	$8	$25
Eternia Playset	$125	$295
Meteorbs		
Cometroid	$8	$20
Ty-Grrr	$8	$20
Astro Lion	$8	$20
Comet Cat	$8	$20
Dinosorb	$8	$20
Tuskor	$8	$20
Crocobite	$8	$20
Orbear	$8	$20
Rhinorb	$8	$20
Gore-illa	$8	$20
1987 Series		
King Randor	$6	$18
Sorceress	$15	$39
Clamp Champ	$6	$18
Blast-Attack	$6	$18
Scare Glow	$6	$18

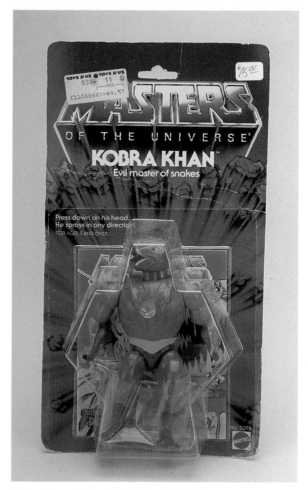

Kobra Khan of the Snake Men. $15-$18 carded. *Courtesy of Play With This.*

Ssqueeze, wife of George Jeffersnake. Think about it. $12-$15 carded. *Courtesy of Play With This.*

The back of Ssqueeze's card shows the various characters in that series.

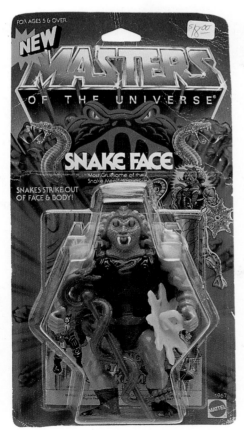

Snake Face, one of the Snake Men. Well I'd hope he's not one of the Teddy Bear Men with a name like that! $12-$15 carded. *Courtesy of Play With This.*

Ninjor	$6	$18
Mosquitor	$6	$18
Snake Face	$6	$15
Sssqueeze	$6	$15
Buzz-Saw Hordak	$18	$39
Faker 2 ("He's back!")	$9	$25
Rotar (rare)	$40	$65
Twistoid (rare)	$25	$60
Tyrantisaurus Rex	$50	$150
Bionatops	$35	$125
Turbodactyl	$20	$75
Tower Tools (Released?)	$7	$18
Cliff Climber (Released?)	$7	$18
Scubattack(Released?)	$7	$18
Laser Power He-Man (movie)	$20	$65
Laser-Light Skeletor (movie)	$20	$65

A revived He-Man failed in 1989. Fans missed the squatting legs. Two-Pack $12-$15. *Courtesy of Play With This.*

The Shuttle Pod was a good example of the new He-Man line, which lacked camp appeal. Now, Pod-A-Saur-Us, with stubby little feet and eyes in front, THAT would be a He-Man vehicle! $10-$12 boxed. *Courtesy of Play With This.*

HE-MAN SECOND VERSION

(Mattel 1989)

He-Man and Villain 2-packs	$8	$15
He-Man	$3	$9
Battle Punch He-Man	$3	$9
Thunder Punch He-Man	$3	$9
Hydron	$2	$8
Spin-Fist Hydron	$3	$9
Flipshot	$2	$8
Missile Armor Flipshot (released?)	$3	$9
Darius (released?)	$3	$9
Nocturna	$3	$9
Vizar	$3	$9
Artilla	$3	$9
Staghorn	$3	$9
Spinwit	$3	$9
Tuskador	$3	$9
Skeletor	$3	$9
Disk Of Doom Skeletor	$3	$9
Battle Blade Skeletor	$3	$9
Flogg	$2	$8
Hook 'Em Flogg (released?)	$2	$8
Hoove	$3	$9
Too-Tall Hoove (released?)	$3	$9
Butt Head (Uhh huh huh)	$4	$12
Quakke	$3	$9
Optikk	$3	$9
Karatti	$3	$9
Kayo	$3	$9
Lizorr	$3	$9
Sagatarr	$4	$15
Astrosub vehicle	$3	$10
Shuttle Pod	$6	$12
Bola Jet	$5	$15
Terroclaw Vehicle	$3	$10
Terrortread Vehicle	$3	$12
Starship Eternia	$12	$40

He-Man had taken the world by surprise.

Oh, sure, sword 'n sorcery movies were a popular genre in the early 1980s, but no one could have expected that a company-generated action figure line that was vaguely based on a popular genre could have been so successful.

My theory has always been that He-Man's success was based on the size of the figures. Kenner's Star Wars series had insured that tiny, barely-posable action figures were the common currency in the 1980s. (Oh, there he goes again.) So when, amongst all these 3-4" figures, came a big, bulky five-inch figure who had to squat slightly just to balance his own weight ...

Well, it made an impact on me, I can tell you!

And although I had been able to resist He-Man and his friends at first, there was no way I could withstand the assault that was to follow. Fantasy figures came essentially two ways: Those that were extremely similar to He-Man and those that went entirely their own way.

Fantasy figures from this era ran the gamut from the high-profile antics of The ThunderCats and Blackstar to the Woolworth's-only independents like Monster Man. But most of the lines you'll read about in this chapter share a common trait—they have lots of figures and accessories that are REALLY WEIRD.

AD&D's Zarak and Elkhorn, $2-$3 each. *Courtesy of Play With This.*

There was a lot of whoop-de-doo at the time about certain toys being an evil influence on our nation's children. Many of the characters in these fantasy lines bore a resemblance to the demonic images out of Hieronymous Bosch and the works of similar artists. Also it didn't help (or hurt, depending on your P.O.V.) that the whole "haunted house" phenomenon, popularized by the Amityville case, had everybody seeing flaming-eyed pigs outside their bedroom windows. Any susceptible person could walk into a toy store circa 1983 and see all manner of demons and goblins sitting on the shelves.

And, as luck would have it, our alphabetical guide begins with a line based on the most evil influence on our youth that the 1980s had to offer—none other than Dungeons and Dragons. Or, specifically...

ADVANCED DUNGEONS AND DRAGONS (1983) was based on the notorious game in which players assumed the roles (i.e. pretended they were) various fantasy characters such as wizards, warriors, princesses and, yes, demons. In spite of parental complaints, the toy line (by LJN) enjoyed fairly successful sales. Regardless of the subject matter, the series was innovative, and it was produced with a much higher quality standard than He-Man and most other fantasy figures of the period. In many ways the Advanced Dungeons and Dragons figures resembled painted role playing miniatures, only larger, and in plastic as opposed to metal.

AD&D's Young Male Titan and Ogre King, each $4-$6 as shown. *Courtesy of Play With This.*

AD&D's Ringlerun and Kelek, $3-$4 each.
Courtesy of Play With This.

AD&D's Raging Roper, one of the weirder AD&D Bendies, $4-$5. *Courtesy of Play With This.*

AD&D's Troglodyte and Minotaur struggle for survival, each $3-$4. *Courtesy of Play With This.*

Another innovation was LJN's deployment of various kinds of figures to round out a series—one which included over six dozen items. In addition to traditional action figures, some characters were "bendies" (rubber figures with wires inside to make them posable). Still others were molded as one solid piece, like a statue. This meant that characters who were too risky an investment as full-blooded action figures could still be marketed as part of the line, since, obviously, an unposable figure is much cheaper to produce than a posable one. The most popular piece today is Tiamat, The Five-Headed Dragon. It's rainbow-colored and kinda plasticy, but collectors just never tire of big monsters.

BATTLE BEASTS (1987) was a rather ridiculous Hasbro offering that benefitted from a clever marketing concept. Instead of relying on individual characters to generate sales, the Battle Beasts were generic, bipedal animal men who each bore a talisman on his chest. (Nothing satanic about animal men with talismans on their chests!) There were three groups: wood, fire, and water. The trick was, the talismans were on heat-sensitive stickers and each character's true nature could only be revealed once he was removed from the package. Sound aggravating? They sold accordingly.

Kenner's BATTLE BRAWLERS were a pair of cool, husky monsters with spring-powered attack features. Crackarm had "bone crushing arms" while Hammertail had a whip-action tail. Their sole purpose was to beat the crap out of each other. Unfortunately, they looked like warrior demons, so many parents shied away. Kenner should have stood behind this concept, or else rethought it and tried again, because big battling monsters always make for great toys.

BLACKSTAR was one of my favorites in college. It was based on a Saturday-morning half hour commer-

cial with a theme of fantasy warriors in an outer space setting. Blackstar and pals were sculpted standing upright, as opposed to the perpetual "where's-the-Immodium" squat of He-Man and his kin. There was an added bonus in that each Blackstar character came with a second figure, a "familiar" for those so inclined. Some characters (mostly good guys) came with a "trobbit" which possibly could be a combination of Troll and Hobbit, but that's a wild guess. The bad guys came with an Alien Demon, which resembled a wingless version of the flying monkeys from *Citizen Kane* (or one of those old movies, I forget which one). Second-series figures have a friction-powered sparking light built into them.

BONE AGE (Kenner 1988) was a stupid line based on a stupid idea—that a bunch of cavemen constructed modern-style vehicles like tanks and jet fighters out of dinosaur skeletons—which were also somehow alive. Characters had names like Zur, Brog, and Crag The

A Troll battles a Metta-Flame, each $3-$4. *Courtesy of Play With This.*

A giant is commanded by a wraith, each $3-$4. *Courtesy of Play With This.*

Clubber. How about Turd or Ugg, as in "Ugg! I don't want it, Mommy!"

CONAN (1984) was part of Remco's ongoing attempt to steal a little of He-Man's thunder. Although supposedly based on the Schwarzennegger film, the assorted Conans did not benefit from his likeness. Nevertheless, if viewed as based on the comic book series (the line did feature villain Thoth-Amon) this line deserves a place in history. And besides, the skull-headed Jewel Thief makes a great addition to any collection.

CRYSTAR was definitely based on a comic book, Crystar, issued by Marvel. This line presented fantasy figures in scale with Star Wars and little G.I.Joe, plus some clever accessory playsets like The Spell of The Evil Wizard. Too bad DC comics didn't contract for figures based on its own crystal character, Amethyst, Princess Of Gemworld. That would really have been something to crow about.

Tyco capitalized on the popularity of dinosaurs with DINO-RIDERS (1989) which pitted the human Dino-Riders against the evil Rulons. The action figures were undistinguished (and that's putting it politely). The dinosaurs themselves were so good, that in the 1990s the Smithsonian Institute rereleased them in toy stores as straight dinosaur replicas.

DRAGONRIDERS OF THE STYX bears the distinction of being by far the most satanic action figure line ever made. Not only do the characters have demonic sounding names (the words "demon" and "devil" appear all over the place) but even the name of the series invokes The Styx, legendary river of the Underworld

Whatever knows fear shrinks from the grasp of this Shambling Mound. $3-$4. *Courtesy of Play With This.*

(and mediocre band). Dragonriders was released in 1984 by a company called DFC (Demonic Forces Cash-in?) and consisted of Star Wars scaled fantasy figures (much like Crystar, which didn't sell either). Most of the figures were nothing special: knights, wizards, ogres. It's in the accessories where things really get scary.

Y'see, the Dragon Riders actually were riders of dragons and demons. Two figures came with mounts—I hesitate to call them "horses." One had a human face (brr) and the other a rooster head, rooster tail, and four rooster feet. Most unsettling of all was the Demon Flyer, a vehicle shaped like a horned, winged demon. Dragon Riders Of The Styx never caught on (probably something to do with eternal damnation) and lingered on store shelves until the late 1980s.

Galoob's INFACEABLES had an innovative concept. Each figure's head was sculpted in a monstrous scowl, but then it was covered with a rubber sheath on which was painted a more benign face. All this was covered by a vacuum-sealed helmet. By pulling the figure's legs down, the rubber sheath would close tightly around the head. This gave the appearance that the pleasant face was changing into the ferocious face, as the sculpted "monster" features emerged through the rubber. Got all that? Well, the design necessary for the trick made the figures stiff and unconvincing overall, and the line died off in the, ahh, face of its poor design.

THE LOST WORLD OF THE WARLORD was Remco's 1983 attempt to topple He-Man. The trick here was that this fantasy line was based on a comic book, *Warlord*, created by DC's own Mike Grell. All other characters in the line were from DC's fantasy

A Male Titan carded $18-$20.
Courtesy of Play With This.

Strongheart
carded $15-$18.
*Courtesy of
Play With This.*

comics, including Arak and Hercules. It made for a very interesting group—licensed characters with identities and marketability of their own, who were sold as He-Man also-rans.

What is especially significant about this series is that it is one of the first 1980s figure lines based on a DC comic. (Ironically, Remco's Sergeant Rock series was also based on a DC comic and was also technically a knockoff—of Hasbro's G.I.Joe.) For fantasy fans, the figures also have the distinction of being superior in detail to He-Man.

MANGLORS were rubbery characters who could be pulled apart and put together in all sorts of combinations. This line, from the obscure CBS Toys, flopped because soft, rubbery figures have no play value as action figures—sort of an art project gone horribly wrong!

THE OTHER WORLD from Arco was a line that fascinated me when it was new, and it's the kind of thing that only becomes a valuable collector's item decades after it's released—when people FINALLY see how cool it is. It consisted of bendy figures about 4" tall who had lots of weapons. Also there were bizarre animal-vehicle hybrids like Froggacuda. The best items in the series were the large adventure sets like The Battle Of Red Lake, which featured several warriors, a giant insect, and a two-headed centaur!

And the thing is, just try and go to a toy show and ask the dealers if they have any Other World figures and playsets—they won't know what you're talking about! Trying to collect the series would be a real ordeal—and THAT'S what makes for collector's items, pal!

SECTAURS, WARLORDS OF SYMBION is another example of a long-neglected line, only this one is finally getting its due. Released by Coleco in 1984, this series featured large 7" insect warriors and flying mounts shaped like armored dragon flies and spiders. The mounts were actually cleverly designed hand puppets a child could operate. Coleco pushed hard, offering a five-episode animated miniseries designed to be televised over the course of a week. They also developed the Sectaurs TV commercials as serialized adventures to build interest. I have no idea why they didn't catch on, perhaps they were just ahead of their time.

SILVERHAWKS was the runt of the litter that produced the marvelous ThunderCats and TigerSharks. The Hawks were much smaller figures than their brethren, and they were difficult to distinguish from one another. They also had the absolute all time stupidest names of any of the LJN anthropomorphic lines—and that's saying something.

SUPER NATURALS incorporated holographic imagery. Figures wore hoods which effectively con-

Ringlerun the Good Sorcerer, $15-$18 carded. *Courtesy of Play With This.*

Kelek, the Evil Wizard, $12-$15 carded. *Courtesy of Play With This.*

tained the holographic image. They had alternating human and monster faces, depending on which way you turned the figure. Like most action figures designed around a gimmick, these failed because the gimmick itself made posability limited.

SUN MAN was an early release from Olmec, now more famous for its action figures of Malcolm X and Martin Luther King, Jr. Sun Man was a He-Man knockoff with a multicultural flair, and was especially targeted at African-Americans and Hispanics. His arch-enemy was the evil Pig-Man. Ironically, Porcine-Americans never protested that their particular group was singled out to portray the villain. The defenseless are irresistible targets for racists.

THUNDERCATS was a wild and wooly (okay, hairy) series that took the fantasy figure concept as far as it could go in the Eighties. Its heroes shunned the human look of He-man for a larger and more feral vein. Equally well-realized were the assorted villains, vehicles, and accessories. My personal favorites are the Astral Moat Monster and Tongue-A-Saurus. But I'll tell ya, that cartoon was the worst piece of drivel ever to come out of the half hour commercial factory. The dialogue was asinine and the characters were ciphers. And that Snarf—I could just strangle that little creep! "Snarf! Snarf!" Come here you little booger! Just

let me get my fingers around that furry little neck of yours...

TIGERSHARKS were the ThunderCats' aquatic cousins. Although similar on the surface, deep down they just weren't inspired.

VISIONARIES were human characters from Hasbro, much like futuristic knights. They were articulated like G.I.Joe but featured holograms on their chest shields—a far smarter use of the gimmick than the Super-Naturals. Not that it sold any better.

Finally, Remco's WARRIOR BEASTS appropriately end our tour of Fantasy Land. Ostensibly He-Man knockoffs, these were wackier and more monstrous than most of the residents of Eternia at the time. In fact, Mattel soon brought out stranger characters to compete with these dinosaur-headed and dragon-headed monstrosities. The Warrior Beasts were designed as a companion line to Remco's Lost World Of The Warlord.

For those of you interested in collecting these items, for the most part, you'll need a lot of luck. Only in recent years has the nostalgia factor aroused the public's consciousness about these awesome fantasy figures. Hopefully, toy dealers will soon be proudly displaying the likes of the ThunderCats, Blackstar, and the Warrior Beasts alongside their better-known contemporaries.

Battle Beasts! BAAATLE BEEEEASTS! $1-$2 each. *Courtesy of J.E. Alvarez.*

Blackstar villains Overlord and Vizir, $5-$7 each with accessories (not shown). *Courtesy of Play With This.*

Even I can't be everywhere at once, so here's a carded Dino-Riders figure, with no Dino. $5-$6. *Courtesy of Play With This.*

FANTASY FIGURES

ITEM	LMC	MIP
ADVANCED DUNGEONS AND DRAGONS (LJN 1983)		
For "Battle Action" versions add 20%		
Fully-articulated characters		
Bowmarc	$9	$18
Deeth	$9	$25
Drex	$7	$18
Elkhorn	$7	$18
Falken	$10	$25
Grimsword	$10	$25
Hawkler	$15	$30
Jorelac	$10	$25
Kelek	$8	$15
Mandoom	$12	$25
Melf	$9	$20
Mercion	$7	$18
Metta Flame	$10	$25
Northlord	$10	$20
Ogre King	$10	$20
Peralay	$8	$20
Pulvereye	$10	$25
Ringerlun	$8	$18

An evil Rulon from Dino-Riders, but no dino. $2-$4. *Courtesy of Play With This.*

Galaxy Fighters...

Galaxy Fighters...

Galaxy Fighters...

And more Galaxy Fighters. These have only been included to give you an idea of what a typical He-Man knockoff looks like and to give you a good laugh. $3-$4 carded. *All Courtesy Of Play With This.*

Skylla	$9	$20
Strongheart	$7	$18
Valkeer	$10	$25
Warduke	$8	$18
Young Male Titan	$10	$20
Zarak	$7	$18
Zorgar	$10	$25
Articulated monsters and mounts		
Behir	$9	$18
Bronze Dragon w/Warduke	$15	$29
Bulette	$8	$18
Carrion Crawler	$5	$10
Cave Fisher	$7	$15
Chimera	$7	$15
Destrier Horse w/Warduke	$14	$28
Dragonne	$9	$18
Evil Nightmare Horse	$9	$22
5-Headed Hydra	$4	$15
Bronze Drahgon	$9	$22
Destrier Horse	$8	$20
Hook Horror	$7	$18
Neo-Otyugh	$6	$18
Nightmare w/Ogre King	$18	$26
Pernicon Wind-Up Power Creature	$5	$15
Raging Roper	$5	$15
Solid Figures, each	$5	$12
Snake Cave Playset	$15	$28
Terrasque Wind-Up Power Creature	$5	$15
Tiamat The Five-Headed Dragon	$50	$125
Fortress of Fangs Playset	$25	$65

BATTLE BEASTS (Hasbro 1987)

Beasts, each	$1	N/A
Beasts in package	N/A	$5
Big Horn Chariot	$5	$15
Deer Stalker Chariot	$5	$15
Tearin' Tiger Chariot	$5	$15
Shocking Shark	$6	$18
Wood Beetle	$6	$18
Blazing Eagle Transport Station	$10	$20
Premium Poster—names all characters	$10	N/A

BATTLE BRAWLERS (Kenner 1986)

Crackarm	$25	$50
Hammertail	$25	$50

BLACKSTAR (Galoob 1983)

Add 25% for figures w/o laser light feature

Blackstar w/Trobbit King	$5	$18
Mara w/Flying Trobbit	$7	$22
Klone w/ Trobbit	$5	$15
Overlord Wizard King w/ Trobbit Magician	$5	$15
Palace Guard w/Demon	$5	$18
Neptul w/Demon	$6	$18
Kadray w/Demon	$5	$18
Tongo w/Demon	$5	$18

Sometimes the off-brand stuff equalled the legitimate. This dragon is from Hong Kong—hey! A Chinese Dragon! $4-$6. *Courtesy of Play With This.*

Before the Super Powers, DC licensed out the Warlord during the fantasy craze. $20-$25. *Courtesy of Play With This.*

Machiste sez, "Where's my cheesesteak?" $15-$18 carded. *Courtesy of Play With This.*

Hercules was another DC character at the time. $20-$25. *Courtesy of Play With This.*

Gargo w/ Demon	$6	
Evil Vizir w/Demon	$7	$22
Lava Loc w/Demon	$7	$22
Muton The Wasp w/Demon	$7	$22
Overlord's Devil Knight	$7	$22
White Knight (Released?)	$8	$25
Trobbit Assortment	$10	$25
Demon Assortment (various colors)	$10	$25
Motorized Battle Wagon	$8	$28
Trobbit Wind Machine	$10	$25
Space Ship	$10	$30
Triton, The Flying Bull	$10	$25
Warlock, Blackstar's Dragon	$10	$25
Ice Castle Playset	$18	$35

CONAN (Remco 1984)
Conan The Warrior	$10	$25
Conan The King	$10	$25
Thoth Amon	$6	$18
Devourer Of Souls	$7	$20
Jewel Theif	$9	$22

CRYSTAR THE CRYSTAL WARRIOR (Remco 1983)
Figures, each	$3	$9
Crystal Dragon	$8	$20
Lava Dragon	$8	$20
Lava Shatterpult	$8	$15
Crystal Shatterpult	$5	$15
Crystal Warrior Battle Set	$8	$15
Crystal Warrior Catapult Set	$8	$15
Magic Of Crystal Adventure set	$12	$25
Spell of the Wizard adventure set	$12	$25
Crystal Castle Playset	$10	$25

DINO-RIDERS (Tyco 1989)
Figures, each	$1	$5
Small Dinosaurs	$4	$15
Medium Sized Dinosaurs	$8	$20
Large Sized Dinosaurs	$10	$30
Tyranosaurus Rex	$20	$40

Brontosaurus	$20	$40

DRAGONRIDERS OF THE STYX (DFC 1984)
Rangar The Warrior	$3	$8
The Wizard	$3	$8
The Black Knight	$3	$8
Guliz The Ogre	$3	$8
The Demon Warrior	$4	$10
Dragon Man	$4	$10
Fantar The Human-Headed Horse	$6	$12
Roozan The Rooster-Headed Horse	$7	$12
Duelin'Devils, each	$4	$8
(Pull-Back Action Skull, Demon, Spectre, Dragon)		
Serpent Rider w/ 2 heads	$7	$15
Skull Sled	$7	$15
Demon Flyer	$10	$25
Mystery Action Dragon	$12	$25

THE INFACEABLES (Galoob 1985)
Iron Lion	$7	$15
Robash	$7	$15
Brainor	$7	$15
Tenvo	$7	$15
Tuskus	$7	$15
Torto The Claw	$7	$15
Crusher Cruiser Vehicle	$7	$15
Horrible Hammer Vehicle	$7	$15
Incredible Thrasher Vehicle	$7	$15

LOST WORLD OF THE WARLORD (Remco 1983)
The Warlord	$8	$25
Hercules	$7	$25
Arak	$7	$20
Machiste	$6	$18
Mikola	$6	$18
Deimos	$6	$18
Warlkord/Horse "War Team"	$12	$28
Machiste w/Horse "War Team"	$10	$25
Mikola w/Horse "War Team"	$8	$20
Journey Through Time Playset w/Warlord	$25	$50

Arak had his own comic, too. $18-$20. *Courtesy of Play With This.*

Leave us not forget the barbarian baddies. Here's Mikola...

... And Deimos, each $15-$18 carded. *Courtesy of Play With This.*

Sectaurs Skito $20-$25 boxed.
Courtesy of Play With This.

MANGLORS (CBS Toys 1983)

ManglordW	$6	$15
Manglosaurus	$10	$20
Manglodactyl	$8	$15
Manglizard (Not Released?)		
Manglodemon (Not Released?)		
Manglodragon (Not Released?)		
Manglor Mountain Playset	$10	$25

NIGHTMARE WARRIORS (MTC 1983)

Skeletons in Historic Warrior Armor each $3		$8
(Captain Kidd, Geronimo, Major Bones, Pancho Villa, Sir Lancelot, Spartacus)		

THE OTHER WORLD (Arco 1983)

Individual figures, each	$4	$10
Friction-powered monsters, each	$5	$15
Deluxe Playsets		
Battle Of The Red Lake	$35	$50
Fighting Glowgons	$20	$35
Castle Zendo Playset	$25	$40

PIRATES OF THE GALAXSEAS (Remco 1984)

Figures, each	$5	$12
(Tattoo, Patch, Peg-Leg, Cutlass, Ribs, Crossbones)		
Treasure Island Playset (Not Released?)		
Adrift At Sea Playset (Not Released?)		

SECTAURS, WARLORDS OF SYMBION (Coleco 1984)

Dargon w/Parafly	$12	$25
Zak w/Bitaur	$12	$25
Mantor w/Raplor	$12	$25
Skito w/Toxcid	$12	$25
Commander Waspax w/Wingid	$12	$25

Silver! Silver! Silverhawks—

Ho!!!!!

Dragonflyer w/Dargon	$20	$45
Pinsor w/Battle Beetle	$25	$40
General Spidrax w/Spiderflyer	$25	$40
Skulk w/Trancula	$25	$40
HYVE Playset	$24	$50

Unreleased Second Series Figures
Bodyball (curls up into a ball)
Nuckles (windup punching arm)
Stellara (#1 female soldier)
Bandor (bolo-whip wielding villain)
Night Fighting Dargon
Night Fighting Spidrax
Unreleased Creatures
Gyrofly (launches insect drones)
Snagg (with built-in snare)
Ax-Back (Spring-out axe from shell)
Strangle Bug (with capture legs)
Rhine-Ox with ramming head)
Swipe (with shooting tongue)
Night Fighter Parafly
Fly Finger (with swivelling launcher)
Crossbow (fires "spore spears")

SILVERHAWKS
Flashback	$5	$15
Stargazer	$4	$12
Bluegrass w/Sideman	$3	$10
Bluegrass w/Hotlick	$8	$20
Buzz Saw	$4	$10
Hardware	$7	$10
Hotwing	$4	$12
Steelheart	$10	$25
Quicksilver	$5	$15
Quicksilver w/Sonic Suit	$12	$28
Copper Kidd w/Mayday	$4	$12

Copper Kidd w/Laser Disc (Released?)		
Condor	$5	$12
Mo-lec-u-lar	$3	$10
Mon-Star	$3	$10
Moon-Stryker	$6	$12
Mumbo-Jumbo	$4	$10
Steelwill w/Stronghold	$5	$12
Steelwill with Laser Spark	$5	$12
Windhammer	$5	$15
Tally-Hawk	$6	$18
Sky Shadow	$10	$24
Sky-Runner	$9	$18
Sprint-Hawk	$9	$18
Copper Racer	$10	$25
Maraj Ship	$10	$30
Stronghold	$8	$18

STEEL MONSTERS (Tonka 1986)
Figures, each	$2	$5

SUN MAN (Olmec 1989)
Figures, each	$3	$6

SUPER NATURALS (Tonka 1986)
Warriors (with legs), each	$3	$6
Ghostlings(short, hooded figures) each	$2	$5
Ghost Finder jeep	$5	$15
Lionwings Flying Lion	$6	$13
Dark Dragon	$5	$15
Tomb Of Doom Playset	$6	$18

THUNDERCATS (LJN 1985)
Lion-O	$15	$40
Ben-Gali	$40	$95
Cheetara	$16	$35

Each about $12-$15 carded. *Courtesy of Play With This.*

Lion-O, the Thunder Cats' mane man, $25-$30 carded. *Courtesy of J. E. Alvarez.*

Cheetara w/ Wilykit	$17	$40
Hachiman	$10	$20
Jaga	$35	$95
Lynx-O	$12	$28
Panthro	$12	$30
Pumyra	$12	$40
Snowman	$12	$30
Tuska Warrior	$12	$30
Tygra	$20	$40
Tygra w/Wilykat	$25	$50
Companions, each	$10	$25
Berbil Bill, Berbil Belle, Berbil Bert, Ma-Mutt, Snarf, Wilykit, Wilykat		
Mumm-Ra	$12	$25
Mumm-Ra Mail-In	$8	$15
Captain Cracker	$12	$25
Captain Shiner	$12	$25
Grune The Destroyer	$12	$25
Jackalman	$10	$20
Mongor	$25	$65
Monkian	$10	$22
Ratar-O	$12	$22
Safari Joe	$10	$22
S-S-Slithe	$12	$20
Vultureman	$12	$20
Hammerhand	$10	$25
Top-Spinner	$10	$20
Cruncher	$10	$20
Ram-Bam	$10	$20
2" figurines, each	$3	$5
Blue Stalker	$8	$15
Flying Claw	$8	$15
Skycutter	$8	$15
Nosediver	$8	$20
Fistpounder	$10	$22
Thundertank	$10	$25
Thunderwings	$8	$20
Stilt Runner	$3	$10

Cheetarah and her wily charge, pair for $18-$20 loose. *Courtesy of J.E. Alvarez.*

Berserker, $10-$12.
Courtesy of J. E. Alvarez.

Mumm-Ra's Tomb Fortress, $65-$75 boxed. *Courtesy of J. E. Alvarez.*

Luna-Lasher	$6	$12
Energy Pack (either color)	$3	$9
Astral Moat Monster	$10	$20
Tongue-a-saurus	$10	$25
Mumm-Ra's Tomb Fortress	$15	$45
Cat's Lair Playset	$14	$45

TIGERSHARKS (LJN 1987)

Mako	$5	$10
Dolph	$5	$10
Lorca	$5	$10
Bronc	$5	$10
T-Ray	$5	$10
Captain Bizarrly	$5	$10
Spike Marlin	$5	$10
Doc Walro w/Gup	$5	$15
Sharkhammer Vehicle	$10	$25

VIKINGS (Remco 1984)

Bjorn (Not Released)
Eric (Not Released)

VISIONARIES (Hasbro 1988)

Figures, each	$3	$7
Capture Chariot w/figure	$7	$12
Dagger Assault Vehicle w/Figure	$7	$15
Sky Claw w/Figure	$7	$18
Lancer Cycle w/figure	$6	$14

VOLTRON (Matchbox 1986)

Standard figures, each	$3	$7
Princess Allura	$5	$10
King Zarkon	$5	$10
For LJN's Voltron robots, see Robots chapter		

WARRIOR BEASTS (Remco 1983)

Human bodies w/monster heads, each	$5	$12
(Skullman, Gecko, Wolf, Snakeman, Craven, Hydraz)		
Beast Man w/Horse "Beast Team")	$10	$20

Panthro, carded, $60-$70. *Courtesy of J. E. Alvarez.*

Slithe and Mumm-Ra in his mummy form, each $10-$12. *Courtesy of J. E. Alvarez.*

Monkeyin' around with Monkian, $10-$12 as shown. *Courtesy of J. E. Alvarez.*

The motion picture *The Terminator* challenged our fevered brains with the horrifying possibility of a future in which mankind will be fighting for survial against a horde of robots.

But in the 1980s there was a battle for survival going on *between* robots—The Transformers had arrived and fought for financial survival against the Go-Bots and a horde of imitators.

Created by the Japanese toy company Takara as an offshoot of their Microman (Micronauts) line, The Transformers eventually made their way to America in 1983. Kids in the US had never see anything like them—seemingly-ordinary objects that could transform via a complicated series of hand maneuvers into cool robot action figures. The earliest Transformers were small cars and audio cassettes, which were soon joined by larger vehicles including race cars and jet planes. The thing that attracted adult collectors as well as kids was the high content of diecast metal incorporated into the characters, which enhanced their robotic look and feel. When you've got an early-model Transformer in your hand, baby, you know you've got something!

Not long after, some of the best-known characters arrived. These were among the largest Transformers up to that time, including Soundwave, Optimus Prime, and Megatron.

In 1985, Hasbro unleashed an animated cartoon and a Marvel comic to explain who every one was and their relationship to each other.

With the setup firmly established, Hasbro was free to release an army of Transformers in all sorts of guises and sizes, from smaller ones costing four or five dollars to the obnoxiously-large automatons who incorporated both electric and electronic gimmicks in their construction. Shockwave emitted two different sounds and lit up.

Trypticon was a robot Tyrannosaurus which walked and lit up and could convert into a battle base. Omega Supreme not only made an impressive, light-up, walking robot but could be broken down into a defense base complete with a tank that looked equally cool whether driving around its racetrack or your kitchen floor ... and was not a bad pizza, either.

Another innovation was the gestaldt robot series, wherein a subset of several related Transformers, such as the Constructicons, could combine into one giant robot. Sometimes there were subsets that didn't join up, but were so cool it didn't matter, like the Dinobots and Insecticons.

The Transformers hit the bigtime with *Transforners: The Movie*, a motion picture created in full animation, as opposed to the limited animation allowed by TV budgets. The stellar voice cast included Judd Nelson, Lionel Stander, Eric Idle, Robert Stack, Leonard Nimoy, and even Orson Welles as the voice of the biggest Transformer of all.

As with Hasbro's other success, G.I.Joe, the Transformers just got bigger and more bizzarre as the years progressed, much like Orson Welles, as a matter of fact. The largest Transformer ever released in the United States hit the market in 1987. This was Fortress Maximus, which stood over two feet tall in its robot form.

Another gimmick that worked, and one which related back to the Micronauts, was the concept of ancillary characters who performed some function in relation to their robot hosts. Headmasters featured Autobots and Decepticons whose heads were actually smaller "pilot" figures. The Target Masters, meanwhile, had weapons which converted into robot familiars. The Power Masters were impressive vehicles whose engine blocks could convert into robots. All of this contributed to a

Brawn with minicar, $22-$25.
Courtesy of J. E. Alvarez.

Defensor $40-$50. *Courtesy of J.E. Alvarez.*

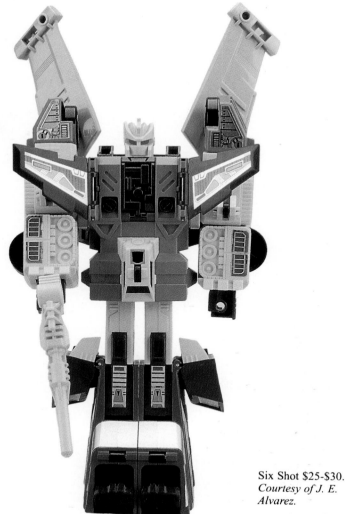

Six Shot $25-$30. *Courtesy of J. E. Alvarez.*

line that Transformers expert Rikki (J.E.) Alvarez succintly describes as "Really bitchen."

Experimentalism was the name of the game as the end of the decade drew near. The Pretenders looked like big fat action figures of human and monster warriors, but were actually shells containing Autobots and Decepticons—thus giving buyers two figures for the price of one. Micromasters gave us tiny, yet still transformable, Transformers. Firecons and Sparkalites incorporated sparking action.

Finally, the Transformers went the action figure route entirely with the Action Masters line—non-transforming action figures of many popular characters, each of whom came equipped with an accessory that transformed!

The sincerest form of flattery, even in the soulless world of robots, is imitation. There were many knockoffs, even ones that used actual molds of real Transformers. A mail-away figure called Reflector turned up as a "camerabot." Grimlock, leader of the Dinobots, found himself recast in gold plastic with extra spikes and a gold tongue in his mouth—and retitled Grimlick!!!

But The Transformers has their share of legitimate competition as well.

Tonka brought the Go Bots over from Japan at about the same time as Hasbro acquired the US rights to the Transformers from Takara. But the Go Bots never had even a tenth of the class that the Transformers had. What Go Bots did have, aside from incredibly, irritatingly juvenile names, was cheapness. That was an area in which the Autobots just couldn't compete. Y'see, Transformers were always a class act—with a price tag to boot. But even the best Go Bots could be had for little money. For a while, Tonka boasted that their Go Bots were some of the best-selling toys of all time—right on the package!

The scenario was similar as well. The Go Bots lived on Go Botron (hyuk) and did battle with evil space marauders called Renegades. The #1 Go Bot leader was named Leader-1 (again, hyuk). There was an offshoot line called Rock Lords, whose cartoon had the coolest theme song of any half-hour commercial at the time. Tonka pushed hard on Rock Lords but the concept didn't really catch on.

Another Japanese-inspired transforming robot craze was the vehicles-that-become-a-robot series. This was imported by LJN as Voltron. A cartoon of Voltron was dubbed into English. For about two years, the mechanical lions that combined to form Voltron were seen on virtually every kind of merchandise. LJN's Lion Bots and Voltrons were in every playground in America. Action figures based on the human characters—without robots—were released by Matchbox. There is also a non-Voltron version of the same robot, marketed as Lion Bot. What most Americans did not know at the time was that this concept was also used for Japanese shows with live actors, with extraordinary costumes and miniatures employed to give life to the robots and vehicles. Eventually, of course, this too found its way over, as Mighty Morphin' Power Rangers.

ROBOTS PRICE GUIDE

Apeface, $40-$45. *Courtesy of J. E. Alvarez.*

ITEM	LMC	MIP
THE TRANSFORMERS (Hasbro 1984)		
Small Cars		
Bumblejumper Bumblebee	$45	$95
Bumblejumper Cliffjumper	$45	$95
Cliffjumper Red Racecar	$10	$40
Cliffjumper Yellow Race Car	$9	$50
Huffer Orange Semi Cab	$10	$40
Windcharger Red Firebird	$9	$40
Brawn Green Jeep	$9	$40
Gears Blue Truck	$9	$40
Cassettes		
Frenzy and Laserbeak, pair	$10	$45
Ravage and Rumble, pair	$10	$40
Standard-Size Cars		
Sunstreaker Yellow Countach	$32	$85
Sideswipe, Red Countach	$28	$75
Hound Jeep	$28	$76
Mirage Indy Car	$28	$75
Bluestreak Blue Datsun	$45	$125
Wheeljack Maserati	$28	$68
Trailbreaker Camper	$28	$68
Bluestreak Silver Datsun	$34	$97
Prowl Police Car	$33	$94
Jazz Porsche	$35	$85
Ironhide Van	$28	$68
Ratchet Ambulance w/cross	$39	$115
Ratchet Ambulance no cros	$28	$68
Jets		
Starscream Grey	$45	$85
Thundercracker Blue	$35	$75
Skywarp Black	$35	$75
Larger Figures		
Optimus Prime	$85	$200
Megatron Walther P-38	$80	$200
Soundwave w/Buzzsaw	$32	$88
Briefcase carry case	$5	$10

Highbrow, $25-$30.
Courtesy of J. E. Alvarez.

Aerielbot Gift Set,
$200-$225. *Courtesy
of J. E. Alvarez.*

Abominus is not so abominable for
$40-$45. *Courtesy of J. E. Alvarez.*

Jetfire, $90-$100. *Courtesy of J. E. Alvarez.*

Megatron, $125-$135. *Courtesy of J. E. Alvarez.*

Carry case 3-D case	$7	$15
Series 2 Mini Cars with Minispies		
Bumblebee Yellow	N/A	$85
Bumblebee Red	N/A	$120
Cliffjumper Yellow	N/A	$75
Clifjumper Red	N/A	$95
Huffer	N/A	$60
Windcharger	N/A	$60
Brawn (new face)	N/A	$60
Gears	N/A	$60
Minicars		
Seaspray Hovercraft	$3	$18
Powerglide Plane	$3	$18
Warpath Tank	$3	$18
Beachcomber Dune Buggy	$3	$18
Cosmos Spaceship	$3	$18
Minispies, each	$15	
(Jeep Buggy, Mazda, Porsche)		
Constructicons, each	$7	$30
Devastator Gift Set	N/A	$250
Insecticons, each	$4	$15
Jumpstarters, each	$4	$12
2nd Series Cassettes, each	$16	$40
Triple Changers, each	$22	$49
Deluxe Insecticons, each	$20	$65
Series 2 Cars		
Skids Le Car	$28	$77
Red Alert Fire Chief	$24	$65
Grapple Crane	$24	$60
Hoist Tow Truck	$24	$65
Smokescreen	$25	$65
Inferno Fire Truck	$22	$60
Tracks Corvette	$39	$75
Series 2 Jets		
Ramjet	$15	$55
Dirge	$15	$55
Thrust	$15	$55
Assorted Series 2		
Optimus Prime, Pepsi Version	$88	$275
Omega Supreme base	$80	$150
Jetfire	$45	$145
Shockwave Laser Gun	$50	$120

Trypticon, $60-$65. *Courtesy of J. E. Alvarez.*

Perceptor	$13	$45
Blaster Tape Player	$14	$40
Deluxe Whirl Helicopter	$60	$135
Deluxe Roadbuster	$45	$95
Dinobots		
Grimlock T-Rex	$29	$66
Slag Triceratops	$22	$60
Snarl Stegasaurus	$18	$39
Swoop Pteranodon	$60	$125
Sludge Brontosaurus	$18	$39
Series 2 Mail-Ins and Other Weird Stuff		
Overdrive Red Car Mail-In	$15	$40
Downshift White Car Mail-In	$15	$40
Camshaft Silver Car Mail-In	$15	$40
Powerdasher #1 Jet	$5	$20
Powerdasher #2 Drill	$15	$45
Powerdasher Mail-In Car	$10	$20
Time Warrior Mail-In Watch	$50	$150
Autoceptor Watch all colors	$10	$35
Deceptor Watch all colors	$10	$35
Listen 'N Fun tape w/red Cliffjumper	$13	$35
Listen 'N Fun tape w/ yellow Cliffjumper	$20	$50
Jazz Cookie Crisp Mail-In	$20	$35
2nd Series Collector briefcase w/band	$6	$15
2nd series round 3-D collector case	$10	$30
Series 3		
Bumblebee w/patch	N/A	$50
Seaspray w/patch	N/A	$20
Powerglide w/patch	N/A	$20
Warpath w/ patch	N/A	$20
Beachcomber w/patch	N/A	$20
Cosmos w/patch	N/A	$20
Wheeler future car	$8	$16
Outback brown Jeep	$8	$16
Tailgate white Firebird	$8	$16
Hubcap yellow race car	$8	$16
Pipes blue semi cab	$8	$16
Swerve red truck	$8	$16
Series 3 Minicars		
Wheelie	$4	$15
Others, each	$3	$12
(Outback, Tailgate, Hubcap, Pipes, Swerve)		
Aerialbots (Add 30% with Patch)		
Air Raid F-14	$8	$25

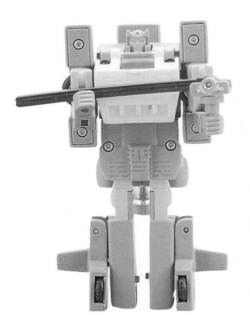

Springer, $20-$25.
Courtesy of J. E. Alvarez.

Piranacon, $45-$55. *Courtesy of J. E. Alvarez.*

Hot Rod, $40-$45. *Courtesy of J. E. Alvarez.*

Perceptor, $12-$15. *Courtesy of J. E. Alvarez.*

Warpath, Cosmos, and Powerglide, each $3-$4. *Courtesy of J. E. Alvarez.*

Skydive F-15	$8	$25
Fireflight F-14 Phantom	$8	$25
Slingshot Harrier Jet	$8	$25
Silverbolt Concorde	$15	$45
Superion Gift Set	N/A	$250
Stunticons (Add 30% with Patch)		
Each	$6	$23
Motormaster tractor trailer	$15	$40
Menasor Gift Set	N/A	$450
Combaticons (Add 30% with Patch)		
Each	$6	$18
Onslaught missile transport	$20	$40
Bruticus Gift Set	N/A	$400
Protectobots (Add 30% with Patch)		
Each	$6	$18
Hot Spot w/Metal Chest	$20	$50
Hot Spot w/plastic chestplate	$145	$40
Defensor Gift Pack	N/A	$400
Battle Charger Runamuck Corvette	$4	$15
Battle Charger Runabout Trans Am	$4	$15
Series 3 Cassettes		
With gold weapons. each	$12	$32
With silver weapons, each	$15	$42
NOTE: Add 10% for figures below with posters		
Triple Changers		
Springer, metal front	$52	$125
Sandstorm metal toes	$25	$50
Broadside	$21	$40
Octane	$21	$40
Heroes Assortment		
Rodimus Prime	$30	$125
Wreck-Car	$25	$70
Series 3 Cars		
Hot Rodd Race Car w/metal toes	$70	$140
Hot Rodd race car plastic toes	$60	$165
Kupp pickup truck w/metal toes	$32	$75
Kupp w/ plastic toes	$32	$75
Blurr	$2	$70
Series 3 Predacons		
Metal Body Versions. each	$40	$75
Plastic Body Versions, each	$25	$55

Brainstorm, $15-$18.
Courtesy of J. E. Alvarez.

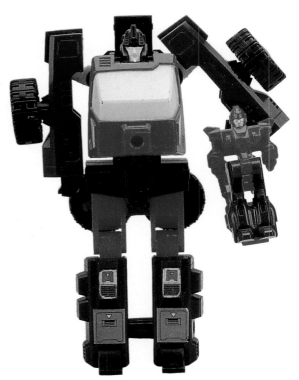

Crosshairs with Pinpointer, $24-$28.
Courtesy of J. E. Alvarez.

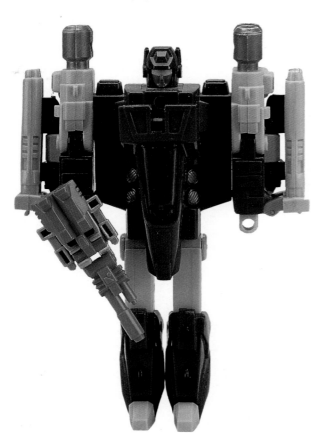

Triggerhappy with Blowpipe, $28-$30.
Courtesy of J. E. Alvarez.

Snapdragon with
Krunk, $18-$20.
*Courtesy of J. E.
Alvarez.*

Metroplex, $25-$30.
Courtesy of J. E. Alvarez.

Gnaw the Sharkticon	$20	$55
Predaking Gift Set (Not Released)		
Series 3 Jets		
Scourge	$22	$65
Cyclonus	$22	$65
Assorted Series 3 Characters		
Reflector camera mail-in	$40	$90
STARS Control Center mail-in	$40	$120
Optimus Prime mail-in	$50	$75
Megatron Mail-in	$70	$100
Galvatron	$40	$100
Ultra Magnus	$22	$60
Trypticon	$65	$165
Sky Lynx	$33	$100
Metroplex with plastic wheels	$25	$75
Metroplex with rubber wheels	$33	$75
Third Series Collectors Showcase	$5	$15
Series Four		
Throttlebots, each	$5	$15
Throttlebots with decoy figures, each	$5	$22
Goldbug Throttlebot w/decoy	$5	$35
Aerialbots with decoys	$10	$28
Stunticons with decoys, each		
Each	$9	$25
Combaticons with decoys, each	$9	$25
Protectobots with decoys, each	$9	$25
Terracons, each	$8	$20
Hun-Grr Dragon	$15	$45
Abominus Terrorcon Gift Set (Not Released)		
Terrorcons w/decoys	$10	$28
Technobots, each	$9	$20
Technobot Scattershot	$15	$45
Computron Technobot Gift Set	N/A	$400
Technobots with decoys	$10	$28
Autobot Decoys loose, each	$2	N/A
Purple Decepticon Decoys, each	$2	N/A
Red Decepticon Decoys, each	$10	N/A
Duocons, each	$6	$20
Series 4 Cassettes		

Above:
Mindwipe $6-$7.
Courtesy of J. E. Alvarez.

Left:
Vorath (Mindwipe's Head) $2-$3. *Courtesy of J. E. Alvarez.*

Optimus Prime, the butt-kickin' top Transformer, $28-$30.
Courtesy of J. E. Alvarez.

Shockwave, Legs Partially Concealed.
$30-$35. *Courtesy of J. E. Alvarez.*

Pretender Optimus Prime, $18-$20.
Courtesy of J. E. Alvarez.

Ratbat and Frenzy	$9	$35
Rewind and Steeljaw	$7	$25
Ramhorn and Eject	$7	$25
Slugfest and Overkill	$4	$18
Clones and Doublespies		
Pounce and Wingspan	$10	$30
Fastlane and Cloudraker	$10	$30
Punch and Counterpunch	$10	$35
Targetmaster Autobots (large size)		
Pointblank with Peacemaker	$28	$60
Sureshot with Spoilsport	$28	$60
Crosshairs with Pinpointer	$28	$60
Kup with Recoil	$57	$115
Blurr with Haywire	$56	$125
Hot Rod with Firebolt	$115	$265
Targetmaster Decepticons (large size)		
Triggerhappy with Blowpipe	$29	$65
Misfire with Aimless	$29	$65
Slugslinger with Caliburst	$35	$74
Cyclonus with Nightstick	$55	$120
Scourge with Fracas	$55	$130
Headmaster Autobots (large size)		
Chromedome with Stylor	$18	$55
Hardhead with Duros	$15	$40
Highbrow with Gort	$15	$40
Brainstorm with Arcana	$15	$40
Headmaster Decepticons (large size)		
Each	$15	$40
Headmaster Horrorcons, each	$20	$55
Monsterbots, each	$12	$35
Assorted Series 4 Figures		
Scorpinok with Lord Zarak	$70	$170
Fortress Maximus	$300	$550
Sixshot	$30	$70

Wreck-Gar, $20-$25. *Courtesy of J. E. Alvarez.*

Left:
Sky Lynx (shuttle section), $15-$18.
Courtesy of J. E. Alvarez.

Below:
Sky Lynx (cargo section), $12-$15.
Courtesy of J. E. Alvarez.

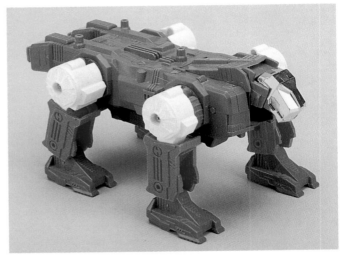

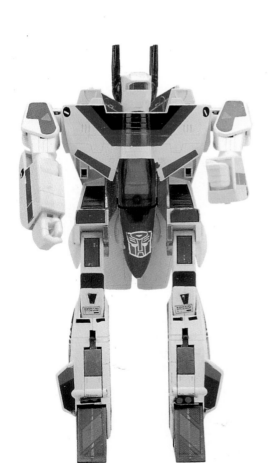

Jetfire, $25-$30. *Courtesy of J. E. Alvarez.*

Superion Gift Set, 5 different guys, $40-$45. *Courtesy of J. E. Alvarez.*

Series 4 mail-ins		
Omnibots, set of 3, all	$45	$120
Thundercracker	$30	$40
Sunstreaker	$20	$30
Wheeljack	$20	$30
Ratchet	$20	$30
Mirage	$25	$35
Series 5		
Sparkabots, each	$3	$8
Firecons, each	$3	$8
Terrorcons, each	$8	$20
Terrorcon Hun-Grrr	$15	$45
Seacons, each	$8	$20
Snaptrap	$15	$45
Piranacon Seacon Gift Set	N/A	$425
Triggerbots, each	$4	$10
Series 5 Cassettes		
Rewind and Steeljaw	$12	$45
Ramhorn and Eject	$12	$45
Squawktalk and Beastbox	$4	$18
Grand Slam and Raindance	$4	$18
Targetmaster Autobots (small series)		
Each	$9	$22
Targetmaster Decepticons (small series)		
Quake with Tiptop and Heater	$9	$37
Spinster with Singe and Hairsplitter	$9	$35
Needlenose with Sunbeam and Zigzag	$9	$42
Headmaster Autobots (Small Series)		
Hosehead with Lug	$15	$35
Siren w/Quig	$15	$35
Nightbeat with Muzzle	$20	$40
Headmaster Decepticons (Small Series)		
Each	$12	$25
Powermaster Autobots, each	$15	$40

Above:
Predaking Gift Set, 5 different guys,
$120-$125. *Courtesy of J. E. Alvarez.*

Right:
Scorponok, $85-$95. *Courtesy of J.
E. Alvarez.*

Powermaster Decepticons, each	$20	$55
Pretenders Large Figure Assortment		
Each	$15	$45
Pretender Beasts Assortment		
Each	$12	$36
Pretender Vehicles Assortment		
Each	$20	$60
Other Series 5 Figures		
Optimus Prime	$30	$70
Scorponok	$55	$175
Doubledealer with Knok and Skar	$25	$60
Quickswitch	$15	$40
Mail-In Figures		
Cosmos	$3	$10
Cliffjumper	$3	$10
Warpath	$3	$10
Set of 3 mini-cars	$10	$30
Series 6		
Micromaster Patrols, each	$4	$8
Micromaster Transports, each	$4	$12
Micromaster Stations, each	$6	$15
Micromaster Bases, each	$10	$30
Pretenders Monster Assortment		
Each	$6	$14
Monstructor Gift Set (Nor Released)		
Pretenders (Small Figures)		
Each	$6	$20
Pretenders Classics		
Each	$10	$30
Mega Pretenders		
Vroom dragster	$10	$30
Thunderwing Jet	$15	$40
Crossblades helicopter	$10	$30

Omega Supreme, with anchovies,
$80-$90. *Courtesy of J. E. Alvarez.*

Omega Supreme in delivery box,
$125-$150. *Courtesy of J. E. Alvarez.*

Gears, Rikki Alvarez' first Transformer,
immortalized forever. $2-$3. *Courtesy
of, gee, I forget!*

Ultra Pretenders		
Each	$20	$50
K-Mart Legends Exclusives		
Bumblebee	$10	$30
Jazz	$10	$35
Grimlock	$15	$45
Starscream	$15	$45
Other Series 6 Figures		
Countdown	$20	$55
Skystalker	$18	$40
Micromaster Combiner Squads		
Each	$6	$12
Micromaster Combiner Transports		
Each	$6	$20
Micromaster Combiner Headquarters		
Anti-aircraft Base	$8	$25
Battlefield Headquarters	$11	$30
Action Masters		
Grimlock with Anti-Tank Cannon	$4	$14
Jazz with Turbo Board	$4	$12
Rad with Lionizer	$4	$10
Rollout with Glitch	$4	$10
Soundwave with Wingthing	$4	$12
Treadshot with Catgut	$4	$10
Devastator with Scorpulator	$4	$12
Krok with Gatoraider	$4	$10
Bubmblebee with Helipack	$4	$14
Blaster with flight pack	$4	$12
Jackpot with sights	$4	$12
Mainframe with Push-Button	$4	$10
Shockwave with Fistfight	$6	$16
Banzai with Razor Sharp	$6	$16
Inferno with Hydro-Pack	$6	$16

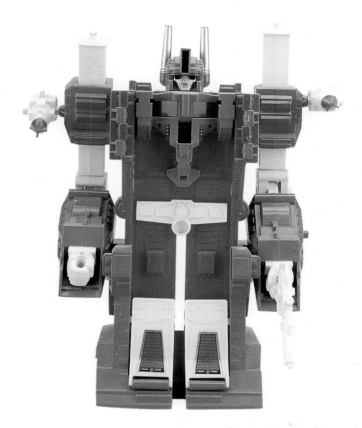

Ultra Magnus, $18-$20, a small price for such an impressive guy. *Courtesy of J. E. Alvarez.*

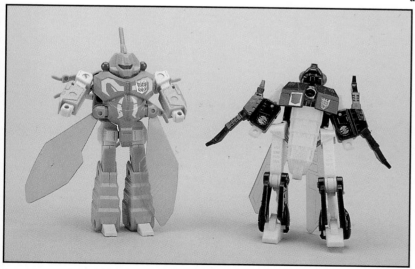

Deluxe Insecticons Barrage ($14-$16) and Ransack ($11-$13). *Courtesy of J. E. Alvarez.*

The one and only Sharkticon, named Gnaw. Aww. $15-$18. *Courtesy of J. E. Alvarez.*

He was Megatron, now he's Galvatron, and he's $28-$30. It's true what they say, name value is everything! *Courtesy of J. E. Alvarez.*

Cyclonus ($18-$20) and Scourge ($18-$20) team up. *Courtesy of J. E. Alvarez.*

Snarl with Tyrannitron	$6	$16
Skyfall with Top-Heavy	$6	$16
Kick-Off with Turbo-Pack	$6	$16
Action Masters Blasters		
Prowl with Turbo Cycle	$8	$20
Axer with Off-Road Cycle	$8	$20
Over-Run with Attack Copter	$8	$20
Starscream with Turbo Jet	$9	$25
Large Action Masters		
Wheeljack with Turbo Racer	$10	$25
Sprocket with Attack Cruiser	$10	$20
Optimus Prime with Truck	$20	$80
Megatron with Tank	$16	$50
Skystalker	$18	$40
Countdown	$20	$55
Gutcruncher with Jet	$12	$40

Optimus Prime, boxed $150-$175. *Courtesy of J. E. Alvarez.*

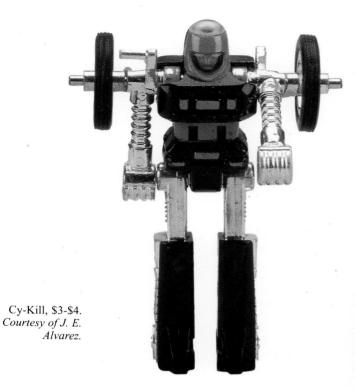

Cy-Kill, $3-$4.
Courtesy of J. E. Alvarez.

THE GO BOTS (Tonka 1985)

Leader-1	$5	$15
Cy-Kill	$5	$15
Others, each	$4	$12
Power suits, each	$3	$9
Collector's Case	$4	$7

Night Ranger, $12-$15. *Courtesy of J. E. Alvarez.*

Pincher, $12-$15. *Courtesy of J. E. Alvarez.*

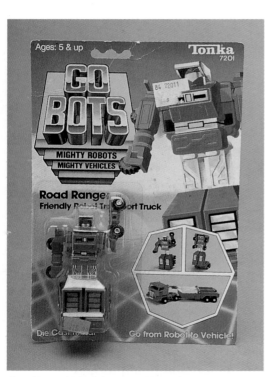

Road Ranger, $12-$15. *Courtesy of J. E. Alvarez.*

Leader-1, $12-$15. *Courtesy of J. E. Alvarez.*

Herr Fiend, $18-$20.
Courtesy of J. E. Alvarez.

A combination ticket! Turbo, $2-$3; Burger King Giveaway, $2-$3;
Leader-1 in TV Show Colors, $2-$3. *Courtesy of J. E. Alvarez.*

Destroyer, $18-$20.
Courtesy of J. E. Alvarez.

Another combination ticket! Tank, $2-$3; Crasher, $2-$3;
and Cop-tor $2-$3. *Courtesy of J. E. Alvarez.*

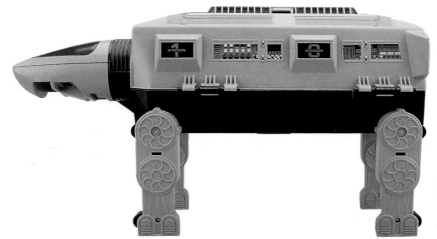

Go Bots Command
Center, $20-$22.
*Courtesy of J. E.
Alvarez.*

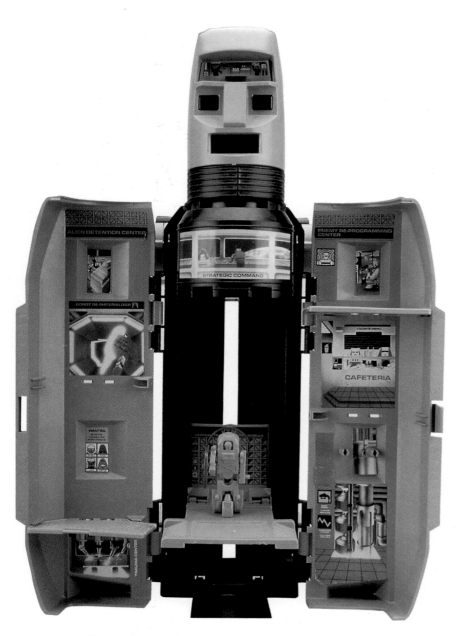

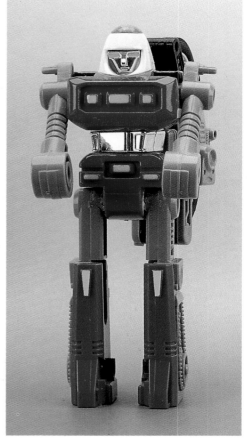

Go Bots Command Center open. *Courtesy of J. E. Alvarez.*

Deluxe Cy-Kill, $6-$7.
Courtesy of J. E. Alvarez.

Rock Lords
Narligator, $5-$6.
*Courtesy of J. E.
Alvarez.*

ROCK LORDS (Tonka 1986)

Figures, each	$2	$7
Narlies Rock Creatures, each	$2	$7
Terra-Roc Flying Monster	$6	$12
Stone Wing Vehicle	$6	$10
Rock Pot Vehicle	$6	$10

VOLTRON (LJN 1986)

Motorized Lionbots, each	$17	$15
Lion Fiorce Fortress	$10	$25
Radio-Controlled Voltron	$28	$50
Battling Black Lion	$6	$18
Voltron Assembler Lion Force	$10	$20
Voltron Assembler Vehicle Team	$10	$20
Voltron Assembler Gift Set	N/A	$35
Lion Force Battle Riser	$6	$12
Vehicle Team Battle Riser	$6	$12
Hydro Cannon	$6	$12
Complete Lionbot Gift Set	N/A	$50
Lionbot Set without Voltron logo	N/A	$50
Complete Vehicle Team Set	N/A	$50

Rock Lords Terra-Rock, $8-$10.
Courtesy of J. E. Alvarez.

And, finally, the aptly-
named Crackpot, $4-$5.
Courtesy of Rikki Alvarez.

The year 1984 was the start of the action figure collector market as we know it today.

In that year, two figure lines premiered that simultaneously attracted both children and adult collectors. Even though adults had been interested in other new figure lines such as Hasbro's revamped G.I.Joe and the various Star Wars series, the double whammy of Kenner's Super Powers collection and Mattel's Marvel Super Heroes Secret Wars line ensured that adult collectors would now be making regular trips to the toy store.

This began a gradual change in the way that action figures were marketed, until, ultimately, some action figure lines became marketed specifically with adults in mind.

It all began when Kenner was looking for a strong property to help build upon its Star Wars success. Kenner's designers approached DC Comics with an idea for a line of super hero figures, each of which had an action feature that duplicated the character's super power. Originally, the designers hadn't quite settled on how the Super Powers' super powers would be activated. Early models had protruding knobs, levers, and wheels. Fortunately, the designers were eventually able to conceal the activator mechanisms inside the figures, thus making them appear perfectly normal on the outside. Thus, The Flash's legs could "run" when his

Super Powers Superman ($12-$15) and Luthor ($6-$8). *Courtesy of Play With This.*

arms were squeezed together, Green Lantern could lift his ring arm up to his power battery, and Aquaman's legs could butterfly kick.

The finished figures also established a new size range, standing between four and five inches tall—head and shoulders above the standard pocket size figures. Another attraction was that many characters were making their first appearances as action figures—Green Lantern, Hawkman, Martian Manhunter, Brainiac, and Mister Freeze to name a few. The Super Powers figures also trundled out the Fourth World characters created by Jack Kirby, making Darkseid the supreme villain of the line, and immortalizing in plastic such characters as Orion and Mister Miracle. The incredibly popular Teen Titans, as revitalized by writer Marv Wolfman and artist George Perez, were represented by Cyborg. His figure arrived so late in the day that the Super Powers line was virtually cancelled the week that Cyborg left the factory, which is why he is so rare today.

When Mattel got wind of Kenner's super-coup, they quickly signed up Marvel Comics and rushed out the Secret Wars collection, loosely based on a popular comic book mini-series which pitted most of Marvel's heroes against her villains. It was during this series that Spider-Man acquired the "living" black costume that eventually transformed Eddie Brock into Venom.

Dr. Fate, $15-$18. *Courtesy of Play With This.*

Clark Kent with rushing-to-work action, $50-$60. *Courtesy of Play With This, Joke Courtesy Jeff Read.*

What really made the Secret Wars line stand out was the amazing, astonishing, incredible awfulness of the entire series, especially in comparison to Super Powers, the line it was intended to compete with. The Secret Wars figures have no action features, and each is equipped with a "secret shield," a cheap plastic accessory containing one of those "flicker" pictures that have one image from the right angle and a different one from the left. The figures themselves sported simplistic five-point articulation at the neck, shoulders, and hips. Their sculpting is not interesting to look at, or suitable to any realistic poses. Many of the figures seem to be made from the same generic body mold, or at the least they share arms, legs, or torsos, painted in different colors. Many details are achieved by rather obvious stickers placed in strategic spots. The regal capes worn by most of the villains simply are not included, which really takes away much of their visual power.

Still, the line was moderately successful because, like the Super Powers series, it introduced many characters who had never been action figures before. It was wise to include Wolverine, the hottest hero in comics at the time, who had been basically ignored as a merchandising cash cow until then.

The accessories were awful. In fact, the helicopter that is passed off as two different vehicles (for Doctor Doom and Captain America) is actually from Mattel's old flop, the Heroes In Action Rescue Corps (1970s).

Collector interest has always been high in three Europe-only released figures of Electro, Constrictor, and Iceman, but the entire line of Secret Wars has been usurped by Toy Biz' 1990s Marvel figures, which are infinitely superior in every way. Aside from a few Secret Wars standouts like The Falcon and Hobgoblin, there is no great collector interest, and prices on Secret Wars remain relatively low.

While Kenner was making DC characters and Mattel was cranking out the Secret Wars collection, Remco decided that it, too, had to have a figure line. Trouble was, all the good super heroes were taken. So Remco settled on some forgotten old Archie Comics super heroes dating back to the 1960s. The line was called The Mighty Crusaders, and featured whistling shields as a ripoff to the Secret Wars characters' secret shields. (Let's face it, if you're gonna rip off a toy line, there are better candidates than one as crappy as Secret Wars.)

When I told my friend Paul Levitt that there was to be a Mighty Crusaders line, he got all exited, because he was thinking of The Mighty Heroes (Strong Man, Rope Man, Diaper Man and Cuckoo Man). But that would have actually been a smart move, and Remco apparently wanted characters that nobody remembered, like The Shield, The Comet, and The Web, and villains like The Buzzard and The Sting. Ironically, the one Archie hero with some name recognition, The Fly, was not produced. As a result, the Mighty Crusaders sold mighty badly, only purchased by collectors looking for inexpensive figures with which to customize their favorite non-produced heroes. Paul himself made a great figure of Mike Baron's The Badger out of The Shield, complete with a thick blob of acrylic paint combed into a head of hair.

The lead villains: Darkseid in blue ($5-$6) and his buddy "Marky" DeSaad ($10-$12). *Courtesy of Play With This.*

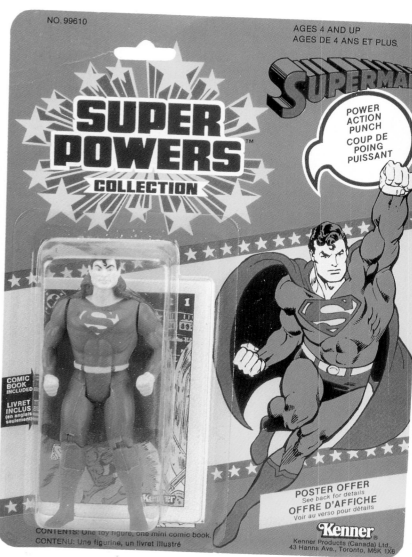

Carded Superman sees his value go, up, up, and— uhh— out. $40-$50. *Courtesy of Play With This.*

Galoob meanwhile was hatching a scheme of their own, and released a Defenders of The Earth line to capitalize on a cartoon show of the same name. This was a team of super heroes made up of King Features comic strip heroes like Flash Gordon, The Phantom, and Mandrake the Magician. I mean, sure, it was a more hopeful resource than the Archie Comics heroes, but what kid of the 1980s wanted a Mandrake The Magician action figure?

The Defenders figures were well-made, but they fell into a trap that Super Powers avoided—their power actions were activated by very visible knobs sticking out of their backs. Still—they were pretty impressive, and the line did give us the first proper action figure of the Phantom. With the mediocre success of the 1996 Billy Zane film, the planned rush on Phantom merchandise never arrived. And so, Phantom fans had to pretend that their Defenders Phantom was Billy Zane, and act out scenes from the amateurish film. ("Slam Evil" indeed. What the hell does that mean?)

By this time, the Super Powers collection was long gone from stores. But it wasn't forgotten. When a relatively-unknown company called Toy Biz decided to get into the action figure game, they snapped up licenses to both the 1989 Batman movie and DC Comics super heroes in general. They proceeded to copy the old Super Powers figures as closely as possible. In fact, many of the prototypes on the back of Toy Biz' 1989 packages look suspiciously like actual Super Powers figures!

But "The Biz" gave itself away in the sculpting of its all-new figures. Riddler was a pinhead and Lex Luthor's punch mechanism causesd him to hit himself repeatedly in the eye. And the less said about Bob The Goon, with his goose-stepping kick and Little Orphan Annie eyes, the better. The new Superman, virtually identical to the Super Powers version, came with a Kryptonite ring. When worn by a human person and held in proximity to Supes, he fell down, weakened by the Kryptonite. How did it work? No one knows, but sales of Supes were slow and most were shipped off overseas for sale.

Other figures cannibalized Super Powers body parts but with new heads or other distinguishing features, like Joker and Penguin. Others are basically knock-offs (how they got away with it I dunno). Mr. Freeze, Wonder Woman, and Robin might as well have come straight from Kenner.

Interestingly, Toy Biz has overcome a very bad start to emerge as the premiere maker of action figures in the 1990s, often setting the standards for Kenner and the rest to follow.

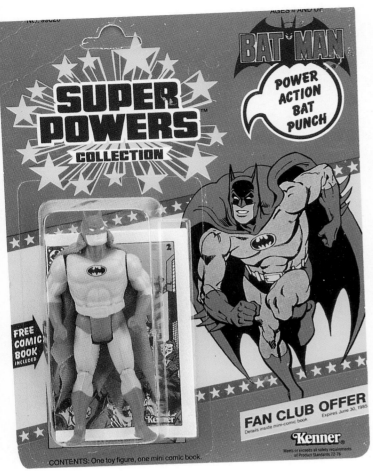

Batman, back when Kenner issued him in his correct colors. $50-$60 carded. *Courtesy of Play With This.*

The Scarlet Speedster can't outrun $20-$25 in cash. *Courtesy of Play With This.*

Whether the night is dark or black, no evil escapes Green Lantern's sight. $50-$60 carded. *Courtesy of Play With This.*

SUPER HERO ACTION FIGURES

ITEM	LMC	MIP
SUPER POWERS COLLECTION (Kenner 1984)		
"Slim cards" are valued at half MIP value		
Superman	$15	$50
Batman	$25	$65
Batgirl (Not Released)		
Robin	$15	$45
Wonder Woman	$10	$40
Aquaman	$17	$50
Flash	$8	$25
Green Lantern	$25	$60
Green Arrow	$25	$60
Firestorm	$12	$29
Hawkman	$22	$70
Martian Manhunter	$18	$39
Red Tornado	$25	$65
Dr. Fate	$18	$75
Plastic Man	$50	$125
Shazam!	$30	$80
Samurai	$40	$100
Cyclotron	$30	$80
Golden Pharaoh	$50	$90
Orion	$25	$70

No. it's not Patty Manterola, it's some other wonder woman. $30-$40 carded. *Courtesy of Play With This.*

Aquaman, brother from the sea, $40-$50 carded. *Courtesy of Play With This.*

Green Arrow, the straight and the narrow, $50-$60 carded. *Courtesy of Play With This.*

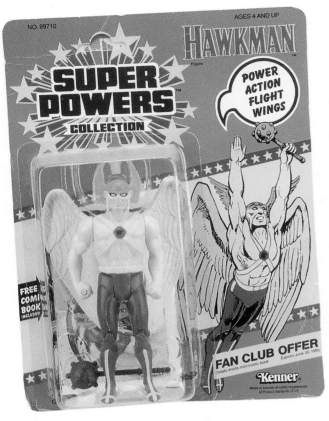

Hawkman wings your way for $60-$70 carded. *Coutesy of Play With This.*

The Joker! $25-$30 carded.
Courtesy of Play With This.

Mister Miracle	$50	$125
Cyborg	$125	$350
Clark Kent (Mail-Away)	$60	$75
Swamp Thing (Not Released)		
The Joker	$12	$30
The Penguin	$15	$50
Mister Freeze	$25	$70
The Riddler (Argentina Only)	$40	$95
Man-Bat (not released)		
Lex Luthor	$8	$22
Brainiac	$12	$28
Darkseid	$6	$18
Kalibak	$5	$18
DeSaad	$12	$25
Steppenwolf (mail away)	$10	$15
Steppenwolf (regular)	$10	$50
Tyr	$35	$65
Mantis	$12	$29
Para Demon	$12	$29
Batmobile	$40	$100
Batcopter	$25	$100
Super Mobile	$15	$40
Lex-Soar 7	$12	$29
Carry Case	$8	$19
Kalibak Boulder Bomber	$12	$25
Delta Probe One	$10	$25
Darkseid Destroyer	$15	$45
Justice Jogger	$10	$20
All-Terrain Trapper (Not Released)		
Hall Of Justice	$45	$150
Darkseid's Tower Of Rage Headquarters (Not Released)		

Everybody's heard about that evil bird they call The Penguin! $40-$50 carded. *Courtesy of Play With This.*

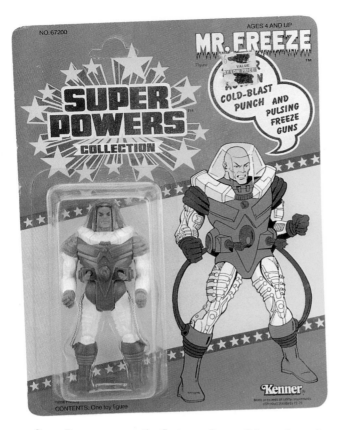

Super Powers gave us the first-ever figure of the cool, cruel Mister Freeze, $60-$70 carded. *Courtesy of Play With This.*

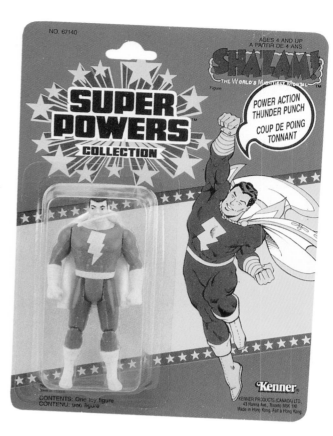

Shazam, Shazam, Shazam, gomer—I mean goes for— $70-$80 carded. *Courtesy of Play With This.*

I only saw Mr. Miracle once when he was new, at the K-Mart in Cinnaminson, NJ. $100-$125. *Courtesy of Play With This.*

Much rarer is the Batcopter, a late release that got minimal shelf time. $90-$100. *Courtesy of Play With This.*

Side view of the rare package. The copter returned—in black—in 1990 as part of Kenner's Batman movie-inspired Dark Knight collection. *Courtesy of Play With This.*

The Justice Jogger. The JUSTICE JOGGER? No invisible plane, no Hawk-Ship, no Batcycle, but we get the JUSTICE JOG-GER. $15-$20. *Courtesy of Play With This.*

The Hall Of Justice had a meeting room, an elevator, even jails for villains. $125-$150 boxed. *Courtesy of Play With This.*

Black costume Spider-Man, $20-$22 as shown. *Courtesy of Play With This.*

MARVEL SUPER HEROES SECRET WARS

Captain America	$8	$22
Iron Man	$8	$22
Daredevil	$15	$35
Falcon	$22	$50
Spider-Man (Red costume)	$15	$35
Spider-Man (black costume)	$22	$65
Wolverine (Black Claws)	$100	$225
Wolverine (Grey Claws)	$25	$75
Iceman (Europe)	$30	$75
Dr. Doom	$8	$22
Dr. Octopus	$8	$22
Kang	$6	$18
Magneto	$6	$18
Hobgoblin	$30	$65
Baron Zemo	$12	$28
Constrictor (Europe only)	$30	$75
Electro (Europe only)	$40	$95
Cap/Doom 2-Pack	N/A	$85
Spidey/Dare/Cap 3-pack	N/A	$95
Doom/Magneto/Kang 3-pack	N/A	$125
Turbo Cycle	$7	$22
Turbo cycle w/hero	$15	$45
Doom Cycle	$7	$22
Doom Cycle w/villain	$15	$45
Turbo Copter	$25	$55
Turbo Copter w/hero	$50	$85
Doom Copter	$30	$65
Doom Copter w/villain	$45	$75
Freedom Fighter H.Q.	$15	$35
Doom Roller	$10	$30
Tower Of Doom	$15	$45
Star Dart Glider w/Spidey	$50	$95
Dark Star Glider w/Doom	$25	$45

"Who loves ya, Bub?" Wolverine (claws not shown) $12-$15 as shown. *Courtesy of Play With This.*

Magneto ($5-$6) and Dr. Doom ($6-$8) show their sinister secret sheilds. *Courtesy of Play With This.*

Kang ($5-$6) and Iron Man ($6-$8) show their shields. *Courtesy of Play With This.*

Iron Man trapped in plastic, $20-$25 carded. *Courtesy of Play With This.*

The Secret Shield in action—a slight turn and viola! Tony Stark, a cool exec with a heart of steel! *Courtesy of Play With This.*

Black costume Spidey carded. $35-$45 as shown. *Courtesy of Play With This.*

Magneto, $4-$5 as shown. Notice the astonishing lack of detail. *Courtesy of Play With This.*

Without his cape, the normally-imposing Dr. Doom looks like a lily to me! As shown, $5-$6. *Courtesy of Play With This.*

Dang! It's Kang! $4-$5 as shown without shield or gun. *Courtesy of Play With This.*

The Doom Cycle, $20-$22 boxed. *Courtesy of Play With This.*

The Doom Roller, an impressive and oppressive war machine, $25-$30 boxed. *Courtesy of Play With This.*

The Doom Roller in action. *Courtesy of Play With This.*

Buddy L released an awesome series of hero-and-cycle combinations. Here's Spidey, $15-$20 boxed. *Courtesy of Play With This.*

Iron Man is ablaze with power—and so's his bike. $15-$18 loose. *Courtesy of Paul Levitt.*

I dunno why the Incredible Hulk needs a cycle, but it makes for a heck of a visual, doesn't it? $25-$30. *Courtesy of Paul Levitt.*

The Web from the Mighty Crusaders. Cool cape, but WHO did you say you were again? $5-$6 as shown. *Courtesy of Play With This.*

"Are you The Brain Emperor?" "No. I am not the—yes! Yes! I am the Brain Emperor!" Try doing Python references under an Aquaman photo. $4-$5. *Courtesy of Paul Levitt.*

He's the Shield, and all those who oppose him must yield. Carded, $10-$15. *Courtesy of Play With This.*

MIGHTY CRUSADERS (Remco 1984)

The Shield	$6	$15
The Fox	$6	$12
The Comet	$6	$18
The Web	$8	$22
The Brain Emperor	$6	$18
The Buzzard	$6	$18
The Sting	$5	$15
The Eraser	$5	$15

DEFENDERS OF THE EARTH (Galoob 1986)

Flash Gordon	$7	$25
The Phantom	$10	$35
Mandrake The Magician	$7	$25
Lothar	$6	$18
Ming The Meriless	$7	$25
Garax	$6	$18
The Phantom's Skull Copter	$12	$29
Flash Gordon's Sword Ship	$12	$29
Garax' Sword Ship	$10	$25
Mongor, Ming's Snake	$15	$33
Claw Copter (Not Released?)		
Gripjaw Vehicle (Not Released?)		

The Fox, whose secret identity is John Marshall, of course. $10-$12 carded. *Courtesy of Paul Levitt.*

Flash! Ahh-ahh saviour of the Universe! $6-$7. *Courtesy of Play With This.*

Garax and his lord Ming The Vase, each $4-$5 as shown. *Courtesy of Play With This.*

Toy Biz' Batman, with a frequently-seen
accessory— a mark-down sticker. $10-$12
carded. *Courtesy of Play With This.*

The back of Batman's card clearly shows a prototype
with a Super Powers head. *Courtesy of Play With This.*

BATMAN/DC COMICS (Toy Biz 1989)

Batman(various faces)	$4	$12
Joker w/forehead curls	$10	$25
Joker no curls	$4	$12
Bob The Goon	$6	$22
Aquaman	$8	$18
Aquaman w/green arms	$5	$15
Flash (DC Comics logo)	$6	$14
Flash (Flash Logo)	$6	$18
Flash with Turbo Platform	$6	$14
Green Lantern	$8	$20
Hawkman	$8	$20
Lex Luthor	$3	$9
Mr. Freeze	$6	$14
Penguin with short missile	$15	$45
Penguin with long missile	$15	$35
Penguin w/ firing umbrella top	$5	$12
Riddler	$7	$15
Robin	$6	$15
Robin packaged with Bob's weapons	$6	$25
Superman	$15	$40
Two-Face	$8	$22
Wonder Woman	$5	$15
Bat Cycle	$10	$25
Joker Cycle	$10	$25
Batmobile with cocoon	$35	$85
Batmobile w/o cocoon	$15	$50
Batwing	$20	$50
Joker Van	$20	$45
Batcave	$25	$60

The Joker looks like Curly did after Moe poked
his cocoanut into the letter press. With curls on
forehead, $20-$25 carded, with clean forehead,
$10-$12 carded. *Courtesy of Play With This.*

Bob The Goon, the world's first Tracey
Walter action figure, with Orphan Annie
eyes and goose step action. $20-$22 carded.
Courtesy of Play With This.

Mr. Freeze is almost a dead ringer for the Super
Powers version, except the—dare I say it—original
has power cords that run from his boots to his thighs.
$12-$14. *Courtesy of Play With This.*

The Batmobile first came with a canopy that simulated the "shields" from the
movie; it was dropped in later versions. $40-$50. *Courtesy of Play With This.*

And now a simple comparison. Here we have the 1989 Robin, who is $12-$15 carded...

And the, ha ha, 1984 "version," $40-$45. Even the package illos are virtual mirror images. *Both Courtesy of Play With This.*

Last, and certainly least, we have the 1989 Lex Luthor, $7-$9 carded. His spring-powered punch allows Lex to sock himself in the eye. "Ooh, I coulda had a V-8!" *Courtesy of Play With This.*

It may seem a little redundant to have a chapter called Kids Stuff in a book about toys. But this chapter is devoted to the kind of cartoony funsters aimed at the under-six crowd, who are weaned on Ninja Turtles to graduate to Ghostbusters and He-Man and finally G.I.Joe and Transformers.

DEFINITELY DINOSAURS! was a fantasy series by Playskool aimed at very young children. The cavemen were as durable as they were chunky, and the dinosaurs, though cartoony, were fully articulated and built to last.

The rest of these figures are self-explanatory, but the Ninja Turtles require some commentary. They were created as a gag by Kevin Eastman and Peter Laird, but their grim adventures (whose look and feel were lifted sustantially from the works of comics artist Frank Miller) caught on unexpectedly with comics readers. As a result, the modest, magazine-sized black and white comic became a cult hit. Eastman and Laird were surprised, almost in disbelief, when they were approached by Surge Licensing. But the wizards at Surge took a property that began as an older-readers satire and turned it into a kiddie-oriented worldwide phenomenon. Kevin Eastman continues to work in comics, and has used his billions to start a foundation to assist struggling comics artists. Peter Laird, presumably, now resides on the island next to Xuxa's.

Scrooge Mc Duck, $6-$8.
Courtesy of Paul Levitt.

Daffy Duck, $8-$9. *Courtesy of Paul Levitt.*

Daffy Duck, $8-$9. *Courtesy of Paul Levitt.*

The Road Runner, $8-$9.
Courtesy of Paul Levitt.

Wile E. Coyote,
forever behind
the eight ball.
$8-$9.
*Courtesy of
Paul Levitt.*

Harpo, Chico, Zeppo, and Shemp, the Teenage Mutant Ninja Turtles, each $6-$8 complete. *Courtesy of J. E. Alvarez.*

Second issue April O'Neil, with the word "PRESS" removed from her outfit. $12-$15. *Courtesy of Play With This.*

Detailed April ($8-$10) and the green version from the News Van ($6-$8). (Note new head.) *Courtesy of Play With This.*

KIDS STUFF ACTION FIGURES

ITEM	LMC	MIP
BABAR THE ELEPHANT (Bikin 1989)		
King Babar	$4	$9
Queen Celeste	$3	$8
Arthur	$3	$8
Flora and Pom, pair	$3	$8
Zephir and Alexander, pair	$3	$8
BARNYARD COMMANDOS		
R.A.M.S.		
Major Legger Mutton	$3	$8
Pilot Fluff Pendleton	$3	$8
Sergeant Wooly Pullover	$3	$8
Other R.A.M.S.	$3	$8
Battle Action RAMS (wind-up)		
Each	$3	$8
P.O.R.K.S.		
Major Piggyback Gunner	$3	$8
General Hamfat Lardo	$3	$8
Other P.O.R.K.S.	$3	$8
Battle Action P.O.R.K.S.	$3	$8
CARE BEARS (Kenner 1984)		
Each	$3	$8
Care Bear Cousins, each	$3	$8
Carry Case	$3	$10
Rainbow Roller Vehicle	$4	$12
Cloud Mobile Vehicle	$4	$12
Care-A-Lot Playset	$10	$20
THE CHIPMUNKS (Ideal 1984)		
Chipmunks, each	$4	$9
David Saville	$5	$15
Chipettes Picnic Buggy	$6	$18
Treat Mobile	$6	$18
Curtain Call Theater	$10	$25
DEFINITELY DINOSAURS! (Playskool 1987)		
Large Dinosaurs, each	$5	$15
Medium Size Dinosaurs, each	$3	$10
Smaller Dinosaurs, each	$2	$10
Cavemen in pairs	$3	$7

Shredder and Splinter, each $6-$8, have a confab on the use of "The Force." *Courtesy of Play With This.*

DISNEY (Arco/Mattel 1986)

Fun Time Mickey	$5	$10
Fireman Mickey	$5	$12
Astronaut Mickey	$5	$12
Pirate Mickey	$5	$10
Rock Star Miniie	$3	$9
Fireman Donald	$5	$10
Cowboy Donald	$4	$10
Farmer Donald	$5	$10
Scrooge McDuck	$8	$18
Carpenter Goofy	$7	$15
Pluto	$6	$12
Clarabelle Cow	$7	$15
Mickey's Safari Adventure Playset	$6	$13
Mickey's '57 Chevy Playset	$6	$13
Wild West Goofy Playset	$6	$12
Goofy's Dune Buggy Playset	$6	$13
Doanld's Speed Boat Playset	$6	$13
Dinosaur Donald Playset	$6	$13
Disney Main Street	$6	$12
Disney Frontierland Playset	$6	$12
Disney Adveutureland Playset	$6	$12
Disney Fantasyland Playset	$6	$12
Disney Tomorrowland Playset	$6	$12

DISNEY CLUBHOUSE COLLECTION (Applause 1987)

Each	$4	$10

Mickey, Minnie, Donald, Daisy , Goofy,
  Pluto

FLINTSTONE KIDS (Coleco 1987)

Figures, each	$3	$9
Vehicle Sets, each	$6	$13
Town Of Bedrock Playset	$10	$20
Bedrock Elementary School Playset	$10	$20
Wind-Ups, each	$3	$8

FLINTSTONES IN ACTION (D-Toys 1985)

Figures, each	$8	$18
Vehicles	$10	$25

FOOD FIGHTERS (Mattel 1988)

Figures, each	$2	$6
Fry Chopper Vehicle	$4	$12
BBQ Bomber Vehicle	$4	$12
Combat Carton Vehicle	$6	$15

Carded Turtles in first-issue packaging bring premium prices, $18-$20 each. *Courtesy of Play With This.*

Bebop ($4-$6) and Foot Soldier ($6-$8). *Courtesy of Play With This.*

Baxter Stockman ($6-$8),
Leatherhead ($8-$10), and
Casey Jones ($6-$8).
Courtesy of Play With This.

Ghengis Frog shows off his
rare yellow belt ($30-$35) to
Ace Duck ($9-$11), and
Usagi Yojimbo ($6-$8).
Courtesy of J. E. Alvarez.

GUMMI BEARS (Fisher-Price 1985)

Figures, each	$3	$8

HOLLYWOOD MICKEY (Arco 1989)

5" figures, each	$4	$10
Figure 3-pack	N/A	$14
Figure 4-Pack	N/A	$18
12" Figures, each	$8	$15

INSPECTOR GADGET (Galoob 1984)

12" figure	$25	$60

LOONEY TUNES (Lucky Bell 1989)

Flocked action figures, each	$5	$9
Gift Sets, each	$4	$10

MADBALLS (AmToy 1986)

Figures, each	$3	$7
Rollercycle w/figure	$5	$10

MICKEY AND FRIENDS (Sears 1988)

Figures, each	$4	$8
Mickey, Minnie, Donald, Daisy, Goofy, Pluto		

POLICE ACADEMY (Kenner 1989)

Figures, each	$3	$7
Vehicles, each	$3	$9
Precinct House	$10	$20

POOH AND FRIENDS (Sears 1988)

Figures, each	$4	$12
Pooh, Tigger, Owl, Kanga, Roo, Rabbit, Eyore, Piglet		

REAL MEN (Mattel 1986)

Half action figure, half finger puppet
(Some were made with Big Jim
 character heads)

Individual Figures, each	$5	$9
Deluxe Sports Sets, each	$6	$12

SANTA MICKEY (Arco 1981)

Santa Mickey	$7	$15

SESAME STREET (Tara 1986)

Figures, each	$4	$12
Gift Set of all seven	N/A	$35

SMURFS (Bikin 1988)

Flocked posable figures, each	$3	$8
Two-Packs	$6	$12
3-Packs	$9	$15
Deluxe Sets	$10	$20

TEDDY RUXPIN (Worlds Of Wonder 1985)

Figures, each	$3	$7

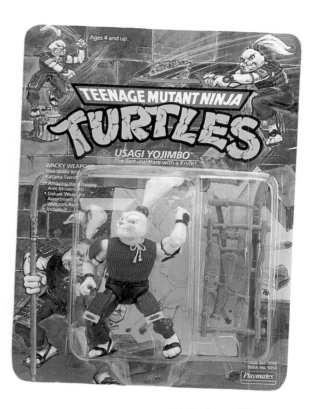

Leatherhead was one of the first hard-to-find characters to develop an inflated aftermarket price. $35-$40 carded on first-issue card. *Courtesy of J. E. Alvarez.*

Stan Sakai's Usagi Yojimbo ("Rabbit Bodyguard") was one of a handful of "indie" characters incorporated into the Turtles universe from other comics. Bob Burden's Flaming Carrot was suggested by Eastman and Laird but turned down by Playmates—a great tragedy. Carded on original card $20-$22. *Courtesy of J. E. Alvarez.*

TEENAGE MUTANT NINJA TURTLES (Playmates 1988)
First Series (MIP Price Doubles w/Fan Club Form)

Donatello	$8	$20
Leonardo	$8	$20
Michaelangelo	$8	$20
Raphael	$8	$20
April O'Neil	$40	$95
Splinter	$8	$25
Shredder	$8	$25
Bebop	$6	$18
Rocksteady	$6	$18
Foot Soldier	$8	$25
Second Series		
April O'Neil, Blue Stripe On Uniform	$10	$25
Ace Duck (wearing hat in package)	$11	$18
Ace Duck (hat off in package)	$11	$35
Genghis Frog yellow belt	$35	$80
Genghis Frog black belt	$6	$16
Krang	$6	$16
Casey Jones	$6	$15
Leatherhead	$10	$40
Metalhead	$5	$14
Rat King	$5	$14
Traag	$4	$12
Usagi Yojimbo	$8	$22
Small accessories, each	$4	$7
Medium-sized accessories, each	$6	$12
Large accessories, each	$10	$16

TOM AND JERRY (Multi-Toys 1989)

Figures, each	$3	$6
Tom, Jerry, Droopy Quackers, Spike, and Tyke		
Large Figure Two-figure Boxed Sets	$8	$16

WUZZLES (Hasbro 1984)

Figures, each	$2	$5

It took decades for the kids who grew up with cartoons to put them into toy lines. Here at last is Droopy, $5-$6 carded. *Courtesy of Paul Levitt.*

First of all, some of you may be saying, "Hey! This is a book about action figures, and those LJN wrestler figures weren't even posable!"

But I make the rules in this playground, and I say, when it comes to playable figures based on licensed characters that were all the rage in the 1980s, you'd have to be insane to skip over LJN's wrestler series.

These guys were big—each around nine or ten inches tall. They were heavy—the average figure weighed in at over a pound. And they were tough. I mean, they were literally tough. One dull August day in 1985, my friend Mark Lumadue and I decided to treat ourselves to some of the wrestlers. I was so impressed by the sturdiness of the one I bought (Iron Sheik) that I threw it down right there in the Cherry Hill Mall parking lot and deliberately rolled over it with my mom's Olds Cutlass. And I tell you folks—not even a scratch!!!

Perhaps some people who spent the 1980s living in the back of a cave, on the planet Odalys in the Vergara System, may not have known that for a few years, wrestling was an unavoidable craze. It took over MTV, our national barometer of American tastes and morays. Cyndi Lauper, who was a singer of

Terry Incredible Hulk Hogan, $12-$15. *Courtesy of Play With This.*

pop music songs, even incorporated some big-name wrestlers into her music video for Steven Spielberg's unforgettable film *THE GOONIES.*

You may notice that I use "wrestling" as a synonym for The World Wrestling Federation, because at that time the WWF *was* wrestling. While it's true that the WCW and others were clawing their way out of the primordial muck, they existed almost as me-too knockoffs of the WWF, both in their TV air time and their merchandising, which only really kicked-in in the 1990s.

So it is that LJN's WWF line stands out as THE collectible wrestling series of the 1980s. It has all the earmarks of a perpetual winner: a stellar cast of heroes and villains, easily-lost accessories, and wipe-away paint jobs that separate the mint condition wheat from the beat-up chaff found at any flea market today. Another aspect in its favor is that the figures get rarer and more valuable the later you go in the series. Only a small handful of characters from the entire second half of the series are worth less than fifty dollars mint in package.

Whatever your preference, they're all here! So enjoy!

Rowdy Roddy Piper, $18-$20. *Courtesy of Play With This.*

Jesse The Body Ventura, $8-$10. *Courtesy of Play With This.*

Andre The Giant (long hair), $12-$15. *Courtesy of Play With This.*

LJN WWF WRESTLERS 1984

ITEM	LMC	MIP
Hulk Hogan (No Shirt)	$15	$40
Rowdy Roddy Piper	$20	$35
Andre The Giant (Long Hair)	$15	$55
Hillbilly Jim	$10	$35
Big John Studd	$10	$30
Iron Sheik	$10	$30
Nicolai Volcoff	$10	$30
Jimmy Superfly Snuka	$15	$40
Junk Yard Dog any color chain	$11	$25
Brutus The Barber Beefcake	$15	$35
George The Animal Steele	$12	$28
Greg The Hammer Valentine	$10	$26
King Kong Bundy	$15	$40
Mr. Wonderful	$10	$25
Andre The Giant (short hair)	$20	$50
Bruno Sammartino	$14	$40
Corporal Kirchner	$10	$22
Don Murraco	$10	$25
Jesse The Body Ventura	$10	$35
Randy Macho Man Savagae	$18	$45
Ricky The Dragon Steamboat	$13	$32
S.D. Jones (either color shirt)	$10	$25
Terry Funk	$14	$30
Tito Santana	$17	$44
Bobby The Brain Heenan	$10	$32

Brutus The Barber Beefcake, $12-$15.
Courtesy of Play With This.

Randy Macho Man Savage, $15-$18.
Courtesy of Play With This.

Captain Lou Albano	$12	$22
Classy Freddie Blassie	$10	$30
Jimmy Hart (with either version megaphone)	$10	$25
Adrian Adonis	$14	$35
The King Harley Race	$55	$175
Kamala The Ugandan Giant	$23	$55
Koko B. Ware	$45	$105
Outback Jack	$12	$25
Ted Arcidi	$12	$35
Billy Jack Haynes	$23	$55
Brett Hart	$70	$325
Jim Neidhart	$50	$230
Brian Blair	$25	$60
Cowboy Bob Orton	$10	$30
Elizabeth	$18	$60
Hercules Hernandez	$16	$40
Jake The Snake Roberts	$21	$58
Jim Brunzell	$17	$75
Mean Gene	$12	$25
Mr. Fuji	$12	$25
Hulk Hogan white shirt	$70	$200
Hulk Hogan red shirt	$95	$290
Johnny V	$14	$30
Ken Petera W.S.M.	$18	$45
One Man Gang	$28	$76
Rick Martel white undies	$30	$120
Tito Santana white undies	$30	$80

George The Animal Steele, $10-$12.
Courtesy of Play With This.

Hillbilly Jim, $8-$10. *Courtesy of Play With This.*

Kamala The Ugandan Giant, $20-$23.
Courtesy of Play With This.

Mr. Wonderful, Paul Orndorff, $8-$10.
Courtesy of Play With This.

Ax	$33	$85
Bam Bam Bigelow	$33	$75
Hacksaw Jim Duggan	$15	$50
Honkey Tonk Man	$25	$60
Refereee any color shirt	$33	$75
Slick	$12	$25
Ted Dibiase M.D.M.	$18	$40
Vince McMahon	$16	$39
Andre the Giant w/black strap	$33	$95
Big Boss Man	$21	$70
Haku	$18	$75
Rick Rude	$21	$50
Warlord	$45	$125
Ultimate Warrior	$95	$260
Sgt. Slaughter Mail-In Exclusive		
(G.I.Joe tie-in) In Shipping Box	$85	$95
Tag Teams		
Hulk Hogan/Hillbilly Jim	N/A	$95
Iron Sheik and Nicolai Volcoff	N/A	$65
Greg Valentine/Brutus Beefcake	N/A	$95
British Bulldogs, pair	$80	$165
Killer Bees, pair	$50	$180
Strike Force boxed	N/A	$225
Hart Foundation boxed	N/A	$525
Wrestling Ring	$25	$45
16" Hulk Hogan	$30	$65
16" Rowdy Roddy Piper	$30	$65
Bendies, each	$5	$12

Jake "The Snake" Roberts, $18-$21.
Courtesy of Play With This.

Magnificent Muraco, $8-$10.
Courtesy of Play With This.

Corporal Kirchner, $8-$10.
Courtesy of Play With This.

Jimmy Snukka, $12-$15.
Courtesy of Play With This.

Vince McMahon, $14-$16. *Courtesy of Play With This.*

Mean Gene, $10-$12. *Courtesy of Play With This.*

Special Delivery Jones, in both shirt variatons,
$8-$10. *Courtesy of Play With This.*

Mr. Fuji, $10-$12. *Courtesy of Play With This.*

Classy Freddie Blassie, $8-$10. *Courtesy of Play With This.*

Bobby The Brain Heenan, $8-$10.
Courtesy of Play With This.

Scott Talis—oops! Captain Lou Albano,
$10-$12. *Courtesy of Play With This.*

The Killer Bees, $50 pair.
Courtesy of Play With This.

Jimmy Hart, the Mouth Of The South,
with notes on his megaphone, $8-$10.
(Also comes with no notes on his
megaphone). *Courtesy of Play With This.*

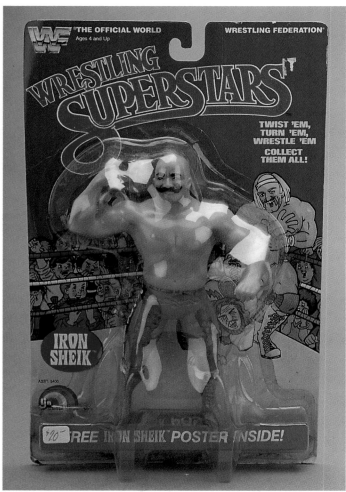

The Iron Sheik
carded, $25-$30
*Courtesy of Play
With This.*

Elizabeth ($15-18) and her buddy Randy Savage. *Courtesy of Play With This.*

Mean Gene carded, $20-$25. *Courtesy of Play With This.*

A 5" bendy figure of Rowdy Roddy Piper, $5-$6. *Courtesy of Play With This.*

115

CHAPTER 9

MOVIE AND TV CHARACTERS

As we all know, licensing has played a part in the action figure industry almost since its inception. No, I take that back. Since before its inception, since proto-action figures like the Hartland series utilized cowboy stars and baseball heroes as the subjects of their lines.

The sixties had James Bond and super heroes, the seventies had more super heroes, and, when Star Wars Fever hit, the world of toy manufacturing learned just how profitable a licensing agreement could be.

And so, in the eighties, virtually anything that could be licensed as an action figure was, pretty much, licensed as an action figure. Here's a look at the various movie and TV tie-ins in alphabetical order.

Galoob took a shot, if you'll pardon the pun, at producing A-TEAM figures in 1984. They were larger than most other figures of the time, standing at a bulky six inches. Plus, each figure came with an entire passle of weapons and accessories (as opposed to half a passle or less, like most figures). The larger size also allowed Galoob's sculptors to achieve decent likenesses of Hannibal (George Peppard), Face (Dirk Benedict), B.A. Baracus (the immortal Mr. T), and Dwight Schultz as "Howling Mad" Murdock. Plus, briefly, there was an Amy A. Allen figure, until the actress who played her got fed up with on-set shenanigans and quit. Galoob blessed the team with a set of four villains, complete with snake-related names inspired by Hasbro's wildly-successful G.I.Joe line.

And speaking of G.I.Joe, Galoob hedged

their bets by producing an A-Team companion line in scale with Hasbro's American heroes. This mini-A Team included all four guys and the four villains as well, plus a wider range of vehicles and accessories than would have been economically feasible for the larger, six-inch figures.

THE ADVENTURES OF INDIANA JONES was a series of pretty unremarkable pocket sized figures from Kenner. It allowed you to recreate the less-boring scenes from "Raiders Of A Lost Art" with playsets based on actual events in the movie. Kenner also took their 12" Han Solo doll, dressed him in a faux leather jacket and floppy hat, and released it as an Indiana Jones doll.

C.H.i.P.s was one of the last attempts at licensing by Mego, the action-figure giant of the 1970s (see that outstanding book, *G.I.Joe And Other Backyard Heroes* by John Marshall, published by Schiffer). When Mego went bankrupt, LJN continued producing some of the C.H.i.P.s figures in the 1980s. The pocket sized line included villains left over from a failed CB-themed series called C.B. McHaul. Of course, *C.H.i.P.s.* star Eric Estrada is far better known as the lead in the Spanish-language soap opera *Two Women, One Road*, which costarred Biby Gaytan, Itati Cantoral, and Laura Leon, and featured the late, lamented Tex-Mex music sensation Selena in a guest-star role. Not surprisingly, Eric Estrada is considered by many to be the Lawrence Olivier of Spanish language TV.

And speaking of Lovable Larry, our next subject is a vehicle in which he starred. It is no surprise that after *CLASH OF THE TI-*

Talking Mr. T from the A-Team, $60-$70.
Courtesy of Play With This.

Pocket size Face and Hannibal, $4-$5 each.
Courtesy of Play With This.

Alternate versions of pocket size Howling Mad Murdock,
each $4-$5. *Courtesy of Play With This.*

TANS, effects maestro Ray Harryhausen decided to semi-retire. *Clash* is an agonizingly boring film, filled with monsters that are pathetic imitations of his previous triumphs. Worst of all is the Kraken, a kind of limp-wristed version of the Ymir from *Twenty Million Miles To Earth*. Despite being a nondescript lump of plastic, the Kraken action figure is the highlight of Kenner's action figure line, and is sought after today mostly for its size and relative rarity. When I was in high school, I used to do a comic called *Superwit*, which was like *Mad*, only funny. I did a satire called "Clash of The Cretins," featuring Percival, the Crackpot, and Penguin the playwright. At the end, when Zeus asks Penguin if men of the future will remember the deeds of the ancient gods, Penguin promises to write a play about the era, a musical called "Greece."

Imperial put out CLASSIC MOVIE MONSTERS in 1986, based on the perennially-popular Universal Studios versions of Dracula, Frankenstein's Monster, The Wolf Man and The Mummy. Although they were basically statues with posable arms, these 9" figures had astounding sculpting, particularly the Dracula. An enormous quantity of Universal Monsters merchandise would be released a few short years later in the early 1990s, some of it highly touted, and none of it approached Imperial's materials in quality.

DALLAS was a proposed Mego line for 1981 that never made it out of the stables. It would have featured versions of all the most popular characters, including J.R., Miss Ellie, Bobby, Sue Ellen, Jock, Pam, and Lucy. A Charlene Tilton action figure—the mind boggles!

Dapol, a company best-known for producing model trains, picked up a license for Britain's longest-running sci-fi series *DOCTOR WHO* in 1988, and the result was available in the U.S. through specialty shops.

They succeeded mightily in reproducing the Doctor's timeship the TARDIS (Time and Relative Dimension In Space) right down to the light up console column that rose and fell as rhythmically as it did on the TV show (although more noisily). Likewise, Dapol's sculpting of the evil Daleks, cybernetic Cybermen (from which Star Trek's Borg are a direct steal), the Ice Warriors (whose "ice lords" were obviously a DIRECT "inspiration" for Darth Vader's appearance and heavy breathing), and the Doctor's robot dog K-9 were all top notch.

But Dapol's handling of the non-robotic characters was appalling.

Even though the figures had pretty good posability, they were seriously lacking in the sculpting department. The first releases of Sylvester McCoy's Doctor, Bonnie Langford's screechy Mel, and the monstrous Tetrap were all virtually unrecognizable. Subsequent additions of Sophie Aldred's Ace and especially Tom Baker's version of the Doctor were downright hideous and over-simplified—Tom Baker was even lacking his trademark scarf!

What really hurt Dapol was its consistent bad timing. If they had hit the ground running with Tom Baker,

Six-Inch Howling Mad Murdock, $6-$8. *Courtesy of Play With This.*

Indiana Jones from the Adventures of Indiana Jones series, $30-$40 as shown. *Courtesy of Play With This.*

K-9, a Dalek and a Cyberman, things would have turned out much better. We can only hope that someday soon a company like Playmates will realize the value of exploiting this internationally-popular license and release a proper line of classic Docs and monsters.

THE DUKES OF HAZZARD (1981) was, like C.H.i.P.s, one of the last great attempts by Mego to cash in on a popular license. It too featured an eight-inch selection of the main characters, and an expanded selection of pocket versions of the residents of Hazzard County. When the *Duke* actors walked, Mego replaced them with Coy and Vance, the cousins. *Dukes* was a truly outstanding show which made an impact on an entire generation and is consistently funny and fun to watch. It's fortunate that James Best survived his encounter with *The Killer Shrews* to play Sheriff Roscoe P. Coltrane. If only Mego had made a Flash figure!

Few people are aware of this, but in 1984, a film came out based on Frank Herbert's classic sci-fi-meets-die-fi novel *Dune*. This led, courtesy of LJN, to the first action figures of Sting and Kyle McLaughlan. Unfortunately, later figures of Lady Jessica and Gurney Halleck were not produced, preventing the world from enjoying the first ever Patrick Stewart action figure. Luckily, prototypes exist of the unreleased figures. The average Trekkie would rearrange his bedroom to display such a rarity.

E.T. was licensed by LJN A.S.A.P. after the film proved a hit, but by the time the stuff arrived on the Q.T. interest was D.O.A. The end result was a handful of accurate and adorable E.T. figurines that didn't sell so hot back then but are rapidly appreciating in value now.

GODZILLA was cast in a new type of rubber—hard rubber—when Imperial released 13" and 6" versions of him in the mid-1980s. They looked even better when painted by the author in the correct deep charcoal grey over that idiotic emerald green. (If anyone would care to tell me which Godzilla movie has a green Godzilla in it, I'd REALLY like to see that motion picture.) There's also a great six-foot inflatable Godzilla, also made by Imperial, that salvaged many a sketch on New Jersey's favorite TV program, *The Uncle Floyd Show.*

THE GREATEST AMERICAN HERO was going to be Mego's best offering of the 1980s, but orders were low, so only the VW Bug with pocket sized Ralph and Bill was released. Prototypes exist of 8" tall, fully-posable figures of Ralph in his super hero suit, Bill, and Pam. A Connie Selleca action figure—the mind boggles!

INDIANA JONES AND THE TEMPLE OF DOOM inspired not one but two—that's TWO—action figure lines, neither of which you probably remember. One was LJN's short-lived series that included Indy, Mola Ram, and Giant Thugee—along with Willie Scott and Short Round, who never made it past the prototype stage. Parental objections over the film's violence (it was the first to be awarded a PG-13, if memory serves) probably kept this line from getting better release. It is ironic that one of the most popular series in film history has had such an awful time of it as an action figure license. The figures based on the first film had lukewarm sales and only

Harry Hamlin as Perseus (ooh, wicked!) $15-$18. *Courtesy of Play With This.*

At $20-$25, Charon really styx it to your wallet. *Courtesy of Play With This.*

one series. The second film's figure line was produced by a relatively-small company and was virtually intercepted before hitting stores. And the third film in the series, even with the previously-figuralized Sean Connery in the cast, had no corresponding action figure line at all!!! The Indiana Jones toy saga is one of the quirkiest elements in the history of 1980s action figures.

Another series of Indy figures was produced for Europe by Star Toys and consists of one Indy figure approximately 8" tall (reports say) which came on an attractive blister card depicting an old map. The three versions were a shirtless Indy with snake, shirtless Indy with alligator, and Indy completely dressed with machine gun. All three versions, however, include his famous hat. Since it was never commercially available in America, I needn't have mentioned it, but samples occasionally turn up at toy collector shows. Did I say "needn't"?

KARATE KID fared a little better, with its figures of Ralph Macchio and Noriyuki "Pat" Morita. Each figure had "Tri-Action" which in English means the figure is capable of three different karate moves. The figures all came with things to break (since breaking things is the purpose of karate). Ironically, most of the package illustrations show the characters in knee-bent poses—positions impossible for figures that did not have knee joints.

Bet you didn't know there were KNIGHT RIDER figures. In 1983, Kenner produced a KITT car with working voice that came with a Michael Knight in scale with Galoob's A-Team goons.

Imperial issued a rubber KING KONG at about eight inches tall but unfortunately never issued one to match their 13" Godzilla.

THE LAST STARFIGHTER from Galoob never made it out of their 1984 product catalog. The line was to have included twelve figures based on the movie, packaged two per card.

THE LEGEND, BRUCE LEE is a legendary Bruce Lee action figure that came out of nowhere in 1983. The figure was about six inches tall and came packaged two ways: with a nunchaku or a bo stick. A series of 2" statuettes was also released by LarGo of Bruce in action poses.

THE LEGEND OF THE LONE RANGER was an attempt by Gabriel to cash in on someone else's attempt to create a new Lone Ranger franchise. Unfortunately, westerns were dead cold in the early 1980s. Probably the best aspect of this release was that, in addition to the pocket-sized line, Gabriel reissued their 1970s triumphs, the 9" Lone Ranger and Tonto figures, along with their horses.

THE LOVE BOAT was one of the lines that helped to sink the battleship Mego in the early 1980s. Figures were made of all characters in the pocket size format, but the ship playset for them was never released. Multi-Toys made an actual playset with small figurines of the

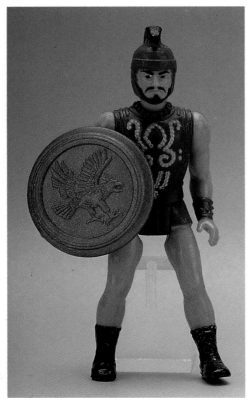

Thallo ain't shallow but he's $15-$18. *Courtesy of Play With This.*

Calibos says, "What's all this talk about demonic-looking toys?" $20-$25. *Courtesy of Play With This.*

crew. But Mego never built a ship for their action figures. I mean, how much fun can a Love Boat crew be without a boat? Then again, how much fun can they be *with* a boat?

Michael Knight wasn't the only fast-car hero on store shelves in the eighties. LJN gave us a MAGNUM, PI playset that combined a Tom Selleck figure and his Ferrari. Magnum was also available separately carded.

Tri-Star International is credited as the producer of a line of pocket-size M*A*S*H figures. Now, this could have come out at any time in the series' eleven year run, but it actually came out just as the show was drawing to a close. The Hawkeye figure did double duty as a blonde-haired generic driver and pilot for the assorted vehicles. There is also an enormous playset.

MAXX FX was manufactured in 1989, but most normal people couldn't find it until 1990 because toy dealers got advance word of it and were buying it up by the caseload. And not without reason. Maxx was to be a Captain Action for the nineties—a fully-posable figure that could be dressed in various guises, with each outfit being sold separately. But instead of becoming super heroes, like Captain Action turned into, Maxx could become movie monsters. The first series was to include dress-up outfits of Dracula, Frankenstein, Freddy Krueger, and the Alien from Alien. But once paternal groups got wind of the gruesome Freddy outfit, they petitioned Matchbox to cease making them. For some reason, rather than proceed with less offensive characters, Matchbox quashed the whole line. The only fully-articulated 10" figure of the 1980s came and went, with only a rumored ten thousand figures produced.

Figures of the singing sensations MENUDO were manufactured by Mego but released by Multi Toys in 1983 after Mego's demise. A Ricky Martin action figure—the mind boggles!

Mattel's MORK AND MINDY line featured 9" figures of Mork and Mindy and, as the 1980s dawned, there was a pocket-size Mork who came with his own eggship.

Ever hear of LewCo? Well, in 1986, they acquired the license for a new Stallone property, *OVER THE TOP*, a film based on the staggeringly-popular sport of professional arm wrestling! It is somewhat ironic that the British use the term "Over The Top" to describe when someone is overacting. The figures were large for their day, about eight inches (in scale to LJN's WWF Wrestlers). Plus there was a 20" Lincoln "Linc" Hawk, the largest action figure made in the 1980s. It couldn't pose in an arm wrestling position, it didn't have any cool accessories, but if you wanted a 20" Sly Stallone—woomp, dey it was!

PEE-WEE'S PLAYHOUSE was based on the inspirational and innovative Saturday-morning TV show. Anyone who knew that Pee-Wee Herman originally rose to fame as the star of a lewd, salaciously-crummy PARODY of that kind of show would not only see the irony of the situation, but would not be surprised by his later trials—literally and figuratively speaking. Fortunately, actor Paul Reubens soon got a grip on things, and has gone on to memorable performances in such high-profile films as *Buffy The Vampire Slayer* and *Batman Returns*.

RAMBO AND THE FORCE OF FREEDOM was an impressive group of chunky 7" action figures based on a cartoon spun off from the movie series. Parental objections to violent themes in toys (which specifically included the melted face of evil character Doctor Hyde) helped clobber this line.

The dreaded Daleks invade the world of Dr. Who in this playset from Dapol, $90-$100. *Courtesy of Paul Levitt.*

E.T. Go Home! $10-$12. *Courtesy of Play With This.*

Michael Knight looks for his car. $6-$8. *Courtesy of Play With This.*

ROBOCOP (Kenner 1989) was based on a half-hour commercial but is close enough in design to the live-action movie version that it belongs in this chapter. In fact, when Toy Island acquired the figure license to the 1990s live-action TV show, they produced their Robocop figure to be in scale with Kenner's left-over villains, still clogging store shelves!

Instead of fighting Rambo's Dr. Hyde, you could have had Stallone fight Mr. T as Clubber Lang from the Phoenix Toys' ROCKY III line. They may have been boxers, but they looked like He-Man knockoffs. There's also a rumored Billy Drago from *Rocky IV*, but I haven't been able to confirm it.

Speaking of action stars, I particularly like the 18" Schwarzennegger that was part of the SCHWAR-ZENNEGGER COMMANDO line, this from Diamond Toymakers in 1985. The giant figure is really cool, and it comes fully-armed. It isn't based on the movie exactly, it's not really based on anything. There is also a He-Man scale line and pocket sized line. In addition to Arnold's Matrix character, there was an assortment of good guys and bad guys that looked to be from some cartoon (a la Rambo). But if there ever was a Commando cartoon, I never heard about it. With no cartoon tie-in, Matrix vanished quickly from stores. Perhaps he retreated back to his mountain cabin where he lived with Alyssa Milano, an arrangement which would be paying off handsomely if it continued through today!

STAR TREK 3: THE SEARCH FOR SPOCK (1984) gave us a good entry in the film series, and gave ERTL a license to manufacture a figure line which came and went rapidly from stores. I doubt they were marketed very well, because there's no reason why they wouldn't have sold. Figures were Kirk, Spock, Scotty, and Klingon Commander Kruge, giving us the first of many Christopher Lloyd action figures, each based on a character that has exactly the same voice as every other character he plays. ERTL was kind enough to include a figure of Kruge's dog puppet as an accessory.

STAR TREK 5: THE FINAL FRONTIER (1989) gave us a mildly disappointing entry in the film series (heh heh) and it was up to Galoob to make money off figures if they could. Galoob decided to produce five eight-inch statues, not aimed at the ten year olds who buy action figures but the older ten year olds who shell out big bucks for anything with Star Trek in it or on it (as opposed to cool people like me, who shell out big bucks for anything with Ultraman monster Red King in it or on it). Which is no reflection on the statues—they're well sculpted and handsomely packaged in window boxes.

But Galoob wasn't done there, because they had also been granted a license to produce figures on the latest franchise, *STAR TREK: THE NEXT GENERATION.* Now, I must say, and I'm going on record here and now as saying, that Galoob's Star Trek figures are the WORST ACTION FIGURES EVER MADE! They look like little indiscriminate blobs. Luckily the packages have photos of the characters on 'em so we know which character each blob is supposed to represent. Even at the time there was much hoopla over the various paint jobs that Data

Garbriel's pocket size Lone Ranger, $15-$18 carded. *Courtesy of Steven Silvia.*

Silver requires about $15-$18 of your own silver. *Courtesy of Steven Silvia.*

came with as he rolled out of the factory. And today, people who have more money than brains pay small fortunes for alternate Datas that have the distinction of being even crappier that the regular Datas.

Galoob released a Shuttle Craft and Ferengi Fighter as one man vehicles for the figures. Three action dioramas were also planned (Bridge, Transporter Room, and Alien Planet) but never released. There is also a bizarre, scaled down Enterprise Bridge Playset. This was a replica of the "saucer section" and contained a bridge with captain's chair, plus navigator and helm stations. It had nifty features like sliding seats, swing-out consoles, and sliding turbolift doors. Although I doubt it was supposed to get past the prototype stage, my pal Nick Delliponti (who loaned out the Data face variations you'll see in nearby photos) swears he handled one at a Kiddie City in Bucks County, Pennsylvania. So it seems there may be a handful of cases that slipped out. Then again, Nick believes in concurrent realities, and may simply be remembering one of those.

STREET HAWK was a 1985 syndicated series about a guy and a motorcycle, kind of a two-wheeled *KNIGHT RIDER* without the news service. But the show didn't last, so Kenner's proposed toy line never made it past the prototype stage. Funskool of India released a Streek Hawk Cycle and rider through their G.I.Joe line.

SUPER STARS from ERTL (1981) was a great idea that strangely never took off. These were 2" metal action figures based on racing superstars (like Richard

Petty) and famous personalities who were car-related (like Colt Seever and The Bandit). There was even a Rocky figure in the line. The Burt Reynolds and Lee Majors figures are identified by their character names, but the Rocky figure has Sly's autograph right on the package.

TARZAN (Dakin 1984) was a semi-tie-in to *GREYSTOKE: THE LEGEND OF TARZAN, LORD OF THE APES* and the line included different Tarzans in various sizes. The 7" version was the largest and best-looking action figure on the market at the time.

TRON (Tomy 1982) gave us pocket sized figures of the movie characters, molded in translucent plastic for that unearthly look that gave audience members such agita when the film was in theaters, and which renders the grainy old prints that they show today on TV totally unwatchable.

UNIVERSAL STUDIOS MONSTERS, released by Remco in 1980, were the last of a, well, a dying breed. These 10" dolls had removable cloth outfits and accordion-like arms for grabbing action. Generally, the figures were indifferently made, although the Wolfman has a great Lon Chaney Jr. likeness and the Phantom is a ghoulish reproduction of Lon's pop. Add a Dracula who looks nothing like Lugosi and a Creature From The Black Lagoon with TEETH, and well, you get the idea. There was, however, a super-cool Monsterizer lab table that lit up. This was followed by a line of MINI-MONSTERS that came in both plain and glow-in-the-dark versions,

a mad scientist lab/crypt playset, and a mini-monsterizer.

The popular TV movie, *V*, was anticipated as a mechandising bonanza. So much so, that a kid in the first movie is actually shown playing with prop action figures of the Visitors. LJN released a 12" Visitor and, overseas, small PVC figurines (see photos). But the proposed action figures of Kyle, Donovan, Diana, and Trooper, and their vehicles, never visited toy stores.

WILLOW was an interesting footnote in action figure history—figures that don't move at all, marketed as action figures! The Willow figure originally included an accessory—a tiny baby piece that was dropped due to laws against small pieces. As everyone knows, the Eborsisk Dragon from the movie (and toy line) was named after Roger Ebert and Gene Siskel.

In 1989, Multi Toys produced a pretty darn thorough WIZARD OF OZ line. This included 12" dolls of all the major characters, but better still there were Munchkins to scale and, at long last, a flying monkey! There was also a line of pocket size versions which, although intended primarily for girls, were as good as most action figures of the period.

ZORRO (Gabriel 1982) was based on the classy Filmation Saturday morning series and provided a very respectable group of pocket size characters and horses.

As impressively as the world of movie licensing had dominated the action figure market in the 1980s, this was nothing compared to the decade ahead!

Buffalo Bill Cody will set you back $15-$18 "just plain" bills, while General George Custer musters up about the same. *Courtesy of Steven Silvia.*

Hawkeye
Pierce. $15-
$18 carded.
*Courtesy of
Play With
This.*

B.J. $15-$18
carded. *Courtesy
of Play With
This.*

MOVIE AND TV CHARACTER ACTION FIGURE LINES

ITEM	LMC	MIP
THE A-TEAM (Galoob 1984)		
6" Figures		
B.A.Baracus	$8	$18
Amy A. Allen	$15	$35
Face	$5	$15
Hannibal	$5	$15
Howling Mad Murdock	$6	$16
Cobra	$6	$18
Python	$6	$18
Rattler	$6	$18
Viper	$6	$18
Gyro Copter w/Murcdock	$18	$35
Attack Cycle w/B.A. Baracus	$22	$45
Pocket Figures		
B.A.Baracus	$5	$18
Hannibal	$5	$15
Face	$5	$15
Murdock	$5	$15
A-Team 4-Pack	$20	$45
Bad Guys 4-Pack	$20	$45
Command Center w/figures	$30	$55
Van w/B.A. Baracus	$18	$35
Jet w/Murdock	$18	$35
Boat w/Hannibal	$18	$35
Corvette w/Face	$18	$35
12" Talking Mr. T	$30	$70
THE ADVENTURES OF INDIANA JONES		
(Kenner 1982)		
Indiana Jones	$50	$175
Toht	$8	$19
Cairo Swordsman	$8	$19
Marion Ravenwood	$85	$225
Indy as German Soldier	$30	$75
Belloq	$25	$65

Colonel Potter.
$15-18 carded.
*Courtesy of Play
With This.*

German Mechanic	$18	$45
Sallah	$19	$55
Belloq in Robe (carded)	$15	$250
Belloq in Robe (mail away)	$15	$25
Horse	$45	$125
Convoy Truck	$25	$75
Map Room Playset	$25	$69
Well Of Souls Playset	$35	$85
Streets of Cairo playset	$25	$69
12" Indiana Jones	$125	$295

Personally, I always sided with Winchester ($8-$10).
Klinger ($6-$8). *Courtesy of Play With This.*

BLUE THUNDER Multi Toys 1983
Helicopter w/figure	$25	$55

C.H.i.P.s (LJN 1983, from Mego originals)
Pocket Size figures
Ponch	$6	$18
Jon	$5	$15
Motorcycle	$8	$25
Gift Set (both figures and cycles)	$25	$55
Cycle and Launcher	$25	$55

CLASH OF THE TITANS (Mattel 1980)
Perseus	$18	$40
Thallo	$18	$40
Calibos	$25	$50
Charon	$25	$50
Pegasus	$22	$65
Pegasus/Perseus Two Pack	$44	$95
Kraken	$50	$150
Bubo Life-Size Figure (not released)		
Playset (not released)		

CLASSIC MOVIE MONSTERS (Imperial 1986)
Dracula	$6	$15
Frankenstein	$6	$15
Wolfman	$6	$15
Mummy	$6	$15

DALLAS (Mego 1981)
Not released

DOCTOR WHO (Dapol 1988)
The Doctor (Grey Coat)	$7	$15
The Doctor (Brown Coat)	$7	$15
Mel (Pink outfit)	$5	$12
Mel (Blue Outfit)	$5	$12
Sophie Aldred as Ace	$9	$22
Tom Baker as The Doctor	$9	$22
K-9	$9	$22
Tetrap	$7	$15
Cyberman	$9	$22
Ice Warrior	$9	$22
Classic Dalek (grey w/blue)	$12	$25

Winchester tried to bring class and distinction to the 4077th, but for all his efforts he's only worth $18-$20 carded. *Courtesy of Play With This.*

Father Mulcahy ($6-$8) ponders a blonde Hawkeye "driver" figure. $5-$6. *Courtesy of Play With This.*

Imperial Dalek (white w/gold)	$12	$25
Daleks (assorted styles	$9	$22
Davros (two hands)	$12	$25
Davros (one hand)	$12	$25
Tardis shell	$18	$30
Tardis Console Playset	$50	$95
Anniversary Playset	$60	$95
Dalek Army w/Davros	$50	$100

DUKES OF HAZZARD (Mego 1981)
8" figures
Bo	$12	$25
Luke	$12	$25
Daisy	$20	$50
Boss Hogg	$15	$28
Coy	$15	$35

Hot Lips Houlihan, the long-suffering heroine. $22-$25. *Courtesy pf Play With This.*

Klinger in a dress. $30-$35. *Courtesy of Play With This.*

Vance	$15	$35
Pocket size figures		
Bo	$8	$18
Luke	$8	$19
Daisy	$12	$25
Uncle Jesse	$12	$25
Cooter	$12	$25
Boss Hogg	$12	$25
Sheriff Roscoe	$12	$25
Cletus	$12	$25
General Lee	$20	$45
Daisy Jeep	$25	$55
Boss Hogg's Cadillac (not released ?)		
Police Car (not released?)		
DUNE (LJN 1984)		
Paul Atreides	$10	$25
Rabban	$10	$25
Baron Harkonnen	$10	$25
Feyd	$10	$25
Stilgar	$10	$25
Sardaukar Warrior	$22	$38
Gurney Halleck (Not Released)		
Lady Jessica (Not Released)		
Spice Scout Vehicle	$15	$35
Sand Worm	$15	$35
E.T. (LJN 1982)		
Walking figure, assorted styles	$10	$25
Action figure, articulated arms and neck		
assorted styles	$12	$28
Spaceship playset w/figure	$28	$55
ET & Elliot powered bicycle	$10	$25
Spaceship Launcher w/fig	$10	$25

GODZILLA (Imperial 1986)		
MIP price= figures with original tags		
13" heavy rubber	$28	$35
13" light rubber	$18	$25
6" figure	$5	$15
inflatable six-footer	$28	$35
THE GREATEST AMERICAN HERO (Mego 1981)		
8" Figures (not released)		
VW Bug w/ Ralph & Bill	$100	$250
INDIANA JONES AND THE TEMPLE OF DOOM (LJN 1984)		
Indiana Jones	$55	$150
Mola Ram	$25	$65
Giant Thugee	$25	$65
Willie Scott (Not Released)		
Short Round (Not Released)		
(Star Toys/Europe/Late '80s)		
Indy w/Jacket	$50	$75
Indy w/crocodile	$45	$70
Indy w/snake	$40	$65
KARATE KID (Remco 1986)		
Daniel	$6	$12
Miyagi	$6	$12
Kreese	$6	$12
Sato	$6	$12
Johnny	$6	$12
Chozen	$6	$12
Attack Alley Training Ctr	$16	$22
Sato's Cannery	$12	$18
Corner Challenge Playset	$12	$22
Competition Center w/figure	$15	$20

Ambulance with blonde Hawkeye driver, $35-$40. *Courtesy of Play With This.*

Jeep with blonde Hawkeye driver, $35-$50. *Courtesy of Play With This.*

KING KONG (Imperial 1985)

8" figure (comes tagged)	$8	$12

KNIGHT RIDER (Kenner 1983)

Knight 2000 Car w/figure	$22	$45
Pocket size figure	$10	$18
6" Figure	$12	$25

LAST STARFIGHTER (Galoob 1984)
Not Released

LEGEND, BRUCE LEE (LarGo 1983)

7" figure, either weapon	$15	$29
2" statuettes, each	$5	$20

LEGEND OF THE LONE RANGER (Garbiel 1982)

The Lone Ranger	$6	$18
Tonto	$6	$18
Butch Cavendish	$6	$18
General George Custer	$6	$18
Buffalo Bill Cody	$6	$18
Silver	$7	$18
Scout	$7	$18
Smoke	$7	$18
Ranger/Silver	$25	$40
Tonto/Scout	$25	$40

Butch/Smoke	$25	$40
Western Town Playset	$35	$55
9" Reissues		
Lone Ranger/Silver	$45	$75
Tonto/Scout	$35	$75

LOVE BOAT (Mego 1981)

Captain Stubing	$5	$12
Doc	$5	$12
Gopher	$5	$12
Isaac	$5	$12
Julie	$5	$12
Vicki	$5	$12
Boat Playset for Figures (Not Released)		

MAGNUM PI (LJN 1983)

Magnum w/Ferrari	$20	$45
Magnum Figure	$10	$22

M*A*S*H (TriStar 1982)

Hawkeye	$6	$18
BJ	$6	$18
Colonel Potter	$6	$18
Hot Lips	$7	$22
Father Mulcahy	$5	$15
Winchester	$7	$22

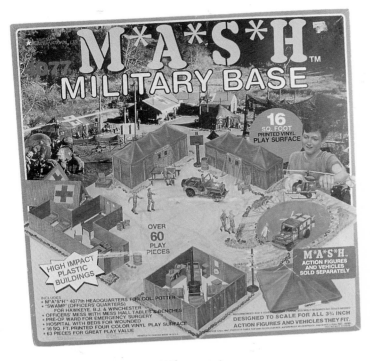

M*A*S*H playset, $50-$60.
Courtesy of Play With This.

Radar's Teddy, easily the best M*A*S*H toy of
all. $30-$40. *Courtesy of Janine Michelle Talis.*

Klinger	$6	$18
Klinger in dress	$12	$35
Helicopter w/Figure	$12	$35
Jeep w/Figure	$12	$29
Ambulance w/Figure	$12	$29
Play Set	$35	$60
MAXX FX (Matchbox 1989)		
Maxx w/Freddy costume	$25	$50
Frankenstein costume (not released)		
Dracula costume (not released)		
Alien costume (not released)		
MENUDO (Multi Toys 1983)		
Ricky Martin	$10	$25
Others, each	$3	$12
MINI MONSTERS (Remco 1983)		
Dracula	$10	$25
Glow Dracula	$10	$25
Frankenstein	$10	$25
Glow Frankenstein	$10	$25
Mummy	$10	$25
Glow Mummy	$15	$45
Phantom	$10	$25
Glow Phantom	$10	$25
Wolfman	$15	$45
Glow Wolfman	$15	$45
Creature	$12	$30
Glow Creature	$12	$30
Monsterizer	$26	$45
Play Case	$12	$30
MORK AND MINDY (Mattel 1980)		
9" Mork	$18	$45
9" Mindy	$15	$40
Pocket Mork w/Egg	$18	$35

Maxx F/X, who, like most great film auteurs, was a short-
lived wonder. $40-$50 boxed. *Courtesy of Paul Levitt.*

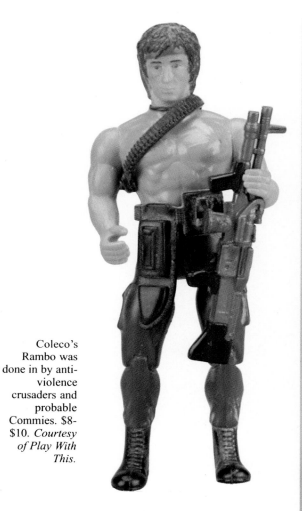

Coleco's Rambo was done in by anti-violence crusaders and probable Commies. $8-$10. *Courtesy of Play With This.*

Robocop carded, $12-$15. *Courtesy of Play With This.*

OVER THE TOP (LewCo 1986)

7" Lincoln Hawks/Stallone	$6	$15
Other 7" Figures	$3	$9
Wrestling Table	$3	$9
2O" Stallone	$20	$45

PEE-WEE'S PLAYHOUSE (Matchbox 1988)

Pee Wee Herman	$9	$18
Miss Yvonne	$6	$15
Cowboy Curtis	$6	$15
King of Cartoons	$6	$15
Reba	$9	$18
Ricardo	$9	$18
Chairry	$6	$15
Globey and Randy	$9	$18
Jambi and Puppet Band	$9	$18
Conky	$9	$18
Magic Screen	$6	$15
Pterri	$9	$18
Pee-Wee w/Scooter	$15	$35
Playhouse Playset	$20	$45

PETER PAN (Sears 1988)
12" Figures

Peter Pan	$6	$18
Wendy	$6	$18
Tinkerbell	$6	$18
Captain Hook	$9	$25

RAMBO (Coleco 1985)

Rambo	$10	$18
Fire Power Rambo	$6	$18
Muscle Power Rambo (Not Released?)		

Chief	$10	$22
Colonel Trautman	$5	$15
Turbo	$6	$12
T.D. Jackson	$10	$22
White Dragon	$5	$15
K.A.T.	$6	$18
General Warhawk	$5	$15
Sargeant Havoc	$5	$15
Black Dragon	$6	$18
Nomad	$15	$35
Gripper	$5	$15
Mad Dog	$5	$15
Dr. Hyde	$9	$22
X-Ray (South America)	$25	$45
Anti Aircraft Gun	$5	$15
Recoilless Anti-Tank Gun	$5	$15
81mm Mortar	$5	$15
.5O Caliber Machine Gun	$5	$15
Defender Assault Vehicle	$12	$25
Skyfire Assault Copter	$12	$25
Skywolf Assault Jet	$12	$25
SAVAGE Strike Cycle	$8	$19
SAVAGE Strike Headquarters	$20	$38
Knockoff 6" Rambo figure (Petroleum-Smelly figure/no leg joints)	$15	$25

ROBOCOP AND THE ULTRA POLICE (Kenner 1989)

Robocop	$5	$15
Birdman Barnes	$9	$21
Anne Lewis	$8	$18
Other Action Figures, each	$4	$16
ED-26O	$12	$28
Robo-1	$15	$39

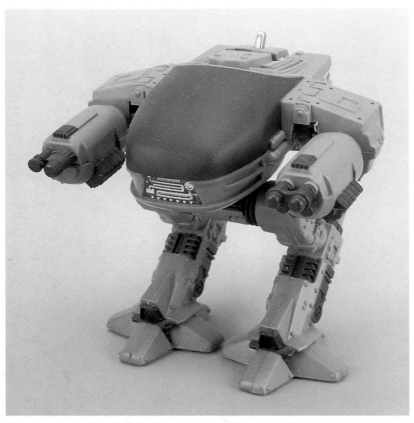

Robocop's arch-foe, ED, $12-$15. *Courtesy of Play With This.*

Nightfighter Robocop glows for you at $12-$15. *Courtesy of Play With This.*

Robo-Cycle	$4	$10
Skull-Hog	$4	$12
Robo-Helmet	$15	$50
Robo-Jailer	$15	$50
Robo-Command	$18	$38
ROCKY III (Phoenix Toys 1983)		
Rocky	$12	$26
Apollo Creed	$12	$26
Mr. T Clubber Lang	$12	$26
Hulk Hogan Thunderlips	$12	$26
SCHWARZENEGGER COMMANDO (Diamond 1985)		
6" Figures		
Matrix (Schwarzenegger)	$18	$35
Other 6" Figures	$5	$10
Pocket Size Figures		
3 3/4" Matrix	$10	$25
All other 3 3/4" figures	$3	$8
18" Matrix	$40	$65
STAR TREK 3: THE SEARCH FOR SPOCK (Ertl 1984)		
Kirk	$18	$40
Spock	$18	$40
Scotty	$25	$55
Kruge	$25	$55
STAR TREK 5 (Galoob 1988)		
Kirk	$18	$40
Spock	$18	$40
McCoy	$18	$40
Sybok	$18	$40
Klaa	$18	$40

"I pity the fool who don't renember me as Clubber Lang in Rocky 3!" says a pint-sized Mr. T., $10-$12 as shown. *Courtesy of Play With This.*

130

7" Arnold from the larger Schwarzenegger: Commando line, $15-$18 as shown. *Courtesy of Play With This.*

Lil' Arnold as Matrix from the pocket sized Schwarzenegger: Commando line, $8-$10 as shown. *Courtesy of Play With This.*

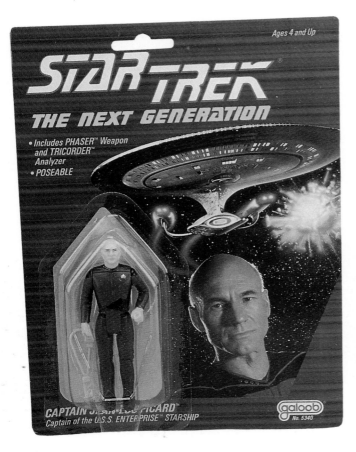

William Riker, who earned the ire of Trekkers everywhere for being tall and handsome, so he's only $18-$20. *Courtesy of Play With This.*

Those of you who live with your parents should recognize Captain Jean-Luc Picard, the Federation's favorite frog. $18-$20. *Courtesy of Play With This.*

STAR TREK: THE NEXT GENERATION
(Galoob 1988)

Picard	$5	$20
Geordi	$5	$20
Worf	$5	$20
Riker	$5	$20
Yar	$9	$25
Data Regular Face	$9	$20
Data Spotted Face	$15	$30
Data Blue Face/Malibu Data	$50	$150
Antican	$30	$70
Selay	$30	$70
Ferengi	$40	$90
Q	$40	$90
Shuttle Gallileo	$35	$75
Ferengi Fighter	$35	$75
Bridge Playset (Released?)		
Diorama Playsets (Not Released)		

SUPER STARS (ERTL 1981)

Sylvester Stallone as Rocky	$10	$22
Colt (Lee Majors)	$9	$18
Bandit (Burt Reynolds)	$11	$25
Richard Petty	$11	$25
Darrel Waltrip	$9	$18

TARZAN (Dakin 1984)

7" Tarzan	$8	$18
4" Tarzan	$6	$18
4" Young Tarzan	$5	$15
4" Kala	$5	$15
Young Tarzan w/Kala	$10	$25

Why is it that black actors on Star Trek always seem to have funny ears or rubber appliances or combs over their eyes? Geordi LaForge $18-$20. *Courtesy of Play With This.*

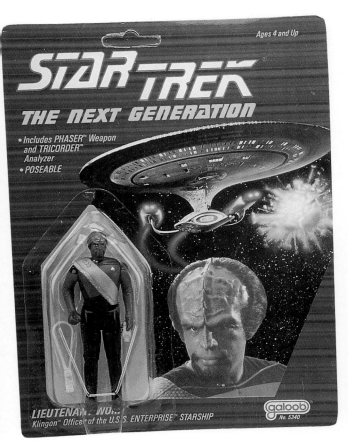

Worf, Worf! $18-$20. *Courtesy of Play With This.*

Commander Data, the little wooden boy. $18-$20. *Courtesy of Play With This.*

I always found it funny that, in a "progressive" show like this, the independent female charcter was named from a sailing term that means "easy to handle." Yar, $20-$25. *Courtesy of Play With This.*

133

Data's regular
face, $18-$20.
*Courtesy of The
Phantom
Windbreaker.*

Data's spotted face. Galoob screws up and now the folks
are paying through their noses to get him. $25-$30.
Courtesy of The Phantom Windbreaker.

Dark-skinned or "Malibu Data." $125-$150 carded.
Courtesy of The Phantom Windbreaker.

Antican must not kill Antican. $60-$70 carded.
Courtesy of Play With This.

Oh, don't be Selay. $60-$70 carded.
Courtesy of Play With This.

Mr. Ferengi will
extract $80-$90 out
of you, which beats a
pound of flesh.
*Courtesy of Play
With This.*

It's Q. that mischievous omniscient being, the Walter Mercado of the galaxies. (Would you believe, the Criswell of The Galaxies? No? Oh, go take "hip" lessons!) $80-$90. *Courtesy of Play With This.*

A closeup of Antican ($25-$30 as shown) and Ferengi ($35-$40 as shown). *Courtesy of Play With This.*

Worf ($4-$5) reasserts that he is not a merry man. Q ($35-$40). *Courtesy of Play With This.*

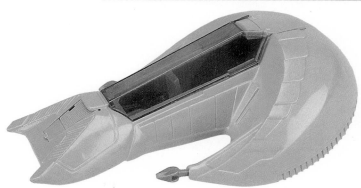

Ferengi Fighter, $30-$35 as shown. *Courtesy of Play With This.*

The Shuttlecraft Galileo, $65-$75 boxed. *Courtesy of Play With This.*

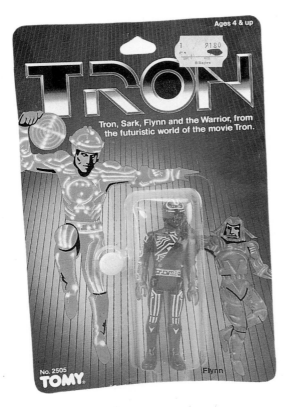

No matter what the color...

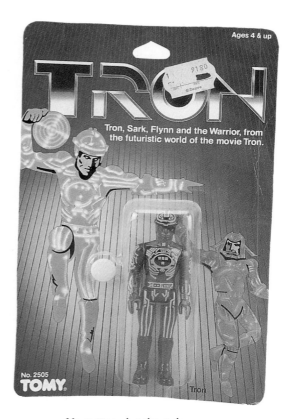

No matter what the style...

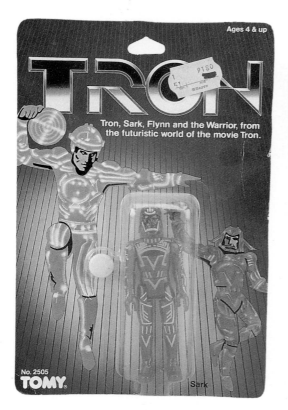

No matter what the names say...

Tron figures go the mile. That wasn't
worth the wait. $15-$18 each carded.
Courtesy of Play With This.

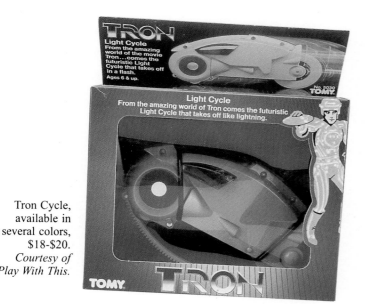

Tron Cycle, available in several colors, $18-$20. *Courtesy of Play With This.*

TRON (Tomy 1982)

Tron	$6	$18
Sark	$6	$18
Flynn	$6	$18
Warrior	$6	$18
Light Cycle (yellow, blue, red)	$8	$22

UNIVERSAL STUDIOS MONSTERS

(Remco 1980)

Frankenstein	$30	$65
Dracula	$35	$75
Wolfman	$45	$95
Mummy	$30	$70
Creature	$75	$250
Phantom	$95	$275
Monsterizer	$50	$150
See also Mini-Monters		

(Imperial 1986)

Dracula	$6	$15
Frankenstein	$5	$12
Wolfman	$5	$12
Mummy	$5	$12

Remco's 9" Frankenstein, available in 1980, was the last of the classic-style acton figures. $25-$30. *Courtesy of Paul Levitt.*

Remco's Wolfman looks just like Lon Chaney Junior—in makeup I mean. $35-$40. *Courtesy of Paul Levitt.*

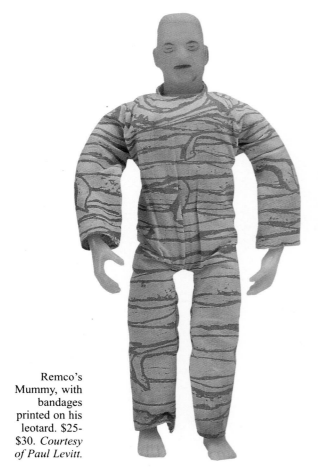

Remco's
Mummy, with
bandages
printed on his
leotard. $25-
$30. *Courtesy
of Paul Levitt.*

More in keeping with the 1980s, Remco released the Mini
Monsters of their 9" characters. Here are Frankenstein ($10-$12)
and Wolfman ($12-$15). *Courtesy of Paul Levitt.*

Remco's mini
Dracula ($10-$12)
and Phantom
($10-$12) show
off their vinyl,
Star Wars-style
capes. *Courtesy of
Paul Levitt.*

Left:
The Mini Monsters play case, $20-$25, provided all the crypt and lab scenarios you needed to make your own monster movies with your Super 8 camera. *Courtesy of Paul Levitt.*

Below:
Toward the end of the decade, Imperial released some not bad 9" posable statues of the classic monsters. Dracula was the best of the lot—graveyard lot, that is. $10-$15. *Courtesy of Play With This.*

One place where sculpted figures are a real improvement is when a cloth leotard simply can't recreate that character's look. Two great examples are the bandages of The Mummy ($10-$12) and the scales of The Creature ($12-$15), both of which look awsome here. *Courtesy of Paul Levitt.*

V (LJN 1985)

12" Visitor	$10	$30
PVC Figurines (Europe)	$8	$25
4" Action Figures & Vehicles (not released)		

WILLOW (Tonka 1988)

Willow w/baby	$2	$5
Willow, no baby	$1	$3
Willow, green shirt (Nestle)	$5	$15
Other figures	$1	$3
Mounted Figures	$2	$5
Heroic Multi-packs	$4	$15
Evil Multi-packs	$5	$15
Catapult (Sears)	$20	$50
Chariot (Sears)	$20	$50
Mangonel (Sears)	$20	$50
Eborsisk Dragon	$20	$40
Nockmaar Castle Playset (Not Released)		

WIZARD OF OZ (Multi-Toys 1989)

12" Figures

Dorothy	$12	$25
Tin Woodsman	$12	$25
Scarecrow	$12	$25
Cowardly Lion	$12	$25
Wicked Witch	$12	$25
Glinda	$12	$25
Boxed set of above	N/A	$95
Wizard	$18	$29

6" Companion Figures

Mayor Munchkin	$12	$25
General Munchkin	$12	$25
Flower Girl Munchkin	$12	$25
Dancer Munchkin	$12	$25
Lolly Pop Munchkin	$12	$25
Witch's Flying Monkey	$18	$29

Pocket Size Figures

Dorothy	$5	$10
Scarecrow	$5	$10
Woodsman	$5	$10
Lion	$5	$10
Glinda	$5	$12
Wicked Witch	$5	$12
Boxed Set	N/A	$65

The V Enemy Visitor often got shelved with the Ken dolls because there were no 12" action figures in 1986. $25-$30. *Courtesy of Play With This.*

ZORRO (Gabriel 1982)

Zorro	$10	$22
Amigo	$10	$22
Captain Ramon	$8	$20
Sergeant Gonzales	$8	$20
Tempest	$9	$20
Picaro	$9	$20

These European V figurines are the closest thing to an acton figure line that the world ever saw. $18-$20 each. *Courtesy of Play With This.*

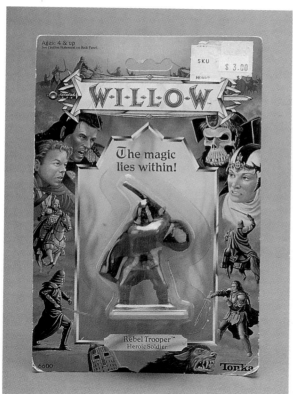

Willow figurines were action figures that didn't move at all. $3-$5. *Courtesy of Play With This.*

A good example of the detail that went into the Willow figure. $2-$3. *Courtesy of Play With This.*

Left:
Carded Zorro, a nice attempt by Gabriel to re-enter the pocket size format. $20-$22. *Courtesy of Steven Silvia.*

Above:
Carded Tempest, $18-$20. *Courtesy of Steven Silvia.*

Picardo, $18-$20 carded. *Courtesy of Steven Silvia.*

Amigo, carded $18-$20. *Courtesy of Steven Silvia.*

Captain Ramon, $18-$20 carded.
Courtey of Steven Silvia.

Sergeant Gonzales, the bumbling foil of Zorro—
and Captain Ramon—comedy-reliefs us out of
this chapter. $18-$20. *Courtesy of Steven Silvia.*

STAR WARS IN THE 1980s

What can I say about the Star Wars phenomenon (Ba Tee Ba Teepee) that hasn't been said already? A lot, probably.

In all honesty, I don't remember much about my viewings of the three films in theaters when they first came out, other than that I'm sure I saw them all. I remember the genuine surprise that I felt when the door opened in Bespin and Darth Vader was standing there; our heroes had been sold out by Lando. And I remember how surprised I was to see Luke's hand cut off, and the dramatic to-be-continued finale of Empire. The only two things I remember about Jedi are the incredible sand skiff fight and the fact that I found the Ewoks so irritating that I cheered whenever they got killed.

Which is not to say that I have something against Star Wars. I don't. I just don't like the action figures.

Empire's Han Solo, $12-$15.
Courtesy of Play With This.

Lando Calrissian in Bespin Fatigues, $10-$12 as shown. *Courtesy of Play With This.*

STAR WARS SEQUELS ACTION FIGURES

Special Price Guide Key To This Chapter:

LMC means "loose, mint, and complete." Item is in like-new condition, with all accessories intact, but no package. As in the rest of this book, this price does NOT reflect the value of a figure in used condition, with no accessories. Those are extremely common and most are only worth a dollar or two. For extremely rare figures, though, you can "figure" on about half the Loose, Mint, Complete price for a used figure with no accessories. ESB means the item is in *Empire Strikes Back* packaging. JEDI refers of course to *Return Of The Jedi* packaging. TL refers to Tri-Logo, the international packaging with material printed in several languages. POTF refers to the limited-release Power Of The Force packaging in which the last figures, and some reissued figures, were marketed.

Also note that this price guide does not include items created prior to 1980 that were reissued for the following movies, such as the Millennium Falcon.

Biker Scout, $8-$10 as shown. *Courtesy of Play With This.*

THE EMPIRE STRIKES BACK

ITEM	LMC	ESB	JEDI	TL
Lando Calrissian	$12	$55	$35	$45
Leia Bespin Gear Profile Shot	$20	$135	$125	
Leia Bespin Gear Front Shot	$110	$75		$95
Add 10% for "crew neck" version				
Han In Hoth Outfit	$15	$55	$45	$45
Luke Bespin Gear, Either Hair Color				
"Walking Shot"	$22	$155		
Luke Bespin Gear, Either Hair Color				
"Looking Shot"	$22	$115	$75	
$120				
Rebel Snow Soldier	$10	$30	$30	$30
Security Guard (White)	$10	$65	$30	$25
Security Guard (Black)	$10	$45	$55	$25
Imperial Snow Trooper	$12	$55	$55	$55
Bossk	$15	$75	$45	$59
FX-7	$10	$45	$38	$59
IG-88	$14	$75	$50	$75

Storm Trooper, $12-$14 as shown. *Courtesy of Play With This.*

Admiral Ackbar, $10-$12 as shown. *Courtesy of Play With This.*

Imperial Snow Trooper, $10-$12 as shown. *Courtesy of Play With This.*

FX-7 Medical Droid, $8-$10. *Courtesy of Play With This.*

Death Star Commander, $15-$18 as shown. *Courtesy of Play With This.*

Item			
21-B	$10	$40	$38	$35
Yoda w/Brown Stick	$25	$65	$65	$55
Yoda w/Orange Stick	$20	$70	$70	$55
Yoda In POTF package $250				
Han In Bespin	$15	$75	$65	$45
Leia In Hoth Gear	$15	$35	$45	$35
Rebel Commander	$10	$22	$22	$27
Ugnaught	$10	$35	$35	$27
Dengar	$10	$35	$35	$27
Lobot	$6	$35	$22	$27
Imperial Commander	$10	$25	$22	$27
AT-AT Driver	$10	$30	$22	$27
Luke In Hoth Gear	$12	$35	$35	$27
Cloud Car Pilot	$19	$45	$45	$27
C-3PO Break Apart (Yaay!)	$8	$35	$30	$25
C-3PO Break Apart (Woo-Hoo) In POTF Package is $88				
R2D2 with scope	$12	$30	$30	$27
AT-AT Commander	$10	$25	$25	$27
Tie Fighter Pilot	$17	$75	$60	$60
Zuckuss	$10	$38	$38	$27
4-LOM	$8	$145	$22	$27

RETURN OF THE JEDI FIGURES

ITEM	LMC	JEDI	TL
Luke Jedi Blue Sabre	$65	$75	$95
Luke Jedi Green Sabre	$45	$75	$65
Luke Jedi in POTF packaging $225			
Leia Boushh Disguise	$18	$45	$28
Lando Skiff Outfit	$14	$35	$16
Chief Chirpa	$10	$22	$18
Rebel Commando	$120	$22	$10
Biker Scout	$14	$25	$14
Biker Scout in POTF Packaging $70			
Empire Royal Guard	$11	$29	$18

Item			
Ree-Yees	$10	$16	$12
Klaatu	$10	$18	$12
Gamorrean Guard	$8	$12	$16
Gamorrean Guanrd in POTF packaging $155			
Nein Numb	$8	$25	$18
Logray	$10	$22	$16
Admiral Ackbar	$10	$22	$16
General Madine	O8	$22	$12
Bib Fortuna	$10	$22	$15
Weequay	$10	$16	$15
Squid Head	$10	$22	$15
Han In Trench Coat	$12	$45	$25
Han In Trench Coat in POTF packaging $280			
Leia in Combat Poncho	$17	$45	$25
Leia in Poncho in POTF packaging $115			
AT-ST Driver	$10	$18	$12
AT-ST Driver in POTF Packaging $65			
B-Wing Pilot	$6	$13	$12
B-Wing Pilot in POTF Packaging $25			
Klaatu in Skiff Outfit	$10	$20	$15
Nikto	$10	$18	$12
Nikto in POTF packaging $275			
8D8	$10	$22	$12
Rancor Keeper	$9	$16	$12
Emperor	$10	$25	$16

R2D2 with sensor scope, $10-$12 as shown. *Courtesy of Play With This.*

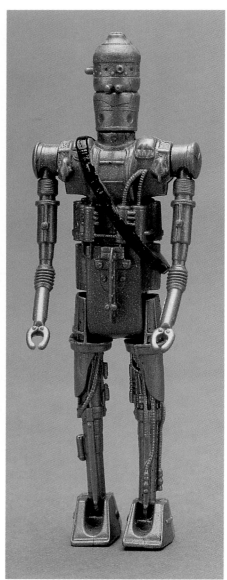

IG-88, $10-$11 as shown. *Courtesy of Play With This.*

Princess Leia in Bespin Gear $15-$17 as shown. *Courtesy of Play With This.*

Emperor in POTF packaging $58

Teebo	$15	$29	$22
Teebo in POTF Packaging $165			
Paploo	$18	$35	$25
Paploo in POTF packaging $45			
Lumat	$18	$33	$25
Lumat in POTF pacakiging $50			
Prune Face	$10	$18	$12
Warrick Wicket	$14	$29	$26
Wicket in POTF packaging $175			
Reebo Band, each	$15	$75	

POWER OF THE FORCE

ITEM	LMC	POTF	TL
Luke In Poncho	$45	$90	$65
R2D2 with pop-up sabre	$80	$150	$105
Han In Carbonite	$115	$235	$185
Luke As Stromtrooper	$150	$350	$240
Lando Gen.	$55	$100	$75
Anakin Skywalker	$35	$700	$64
Imperial Gunner	$95	$160	$140
Warok	$25	$50	$35
Imperial Dignitary	$35	$75	$50
Romba	$25	$55	$35
Barada	$45	$100	$65
A-Wing Pilot	$45	$95	$65
Amanaman (Ba Tee, Ba Teepee)	$90	$215	$140
Yak Face	$140	$800	$275
EV-9D9	$70	$130	$95

Princess Leia in
Endor Gear
Combat
Poncho, $10-
$11 as shown.
*Courtesy of
Play With This.*

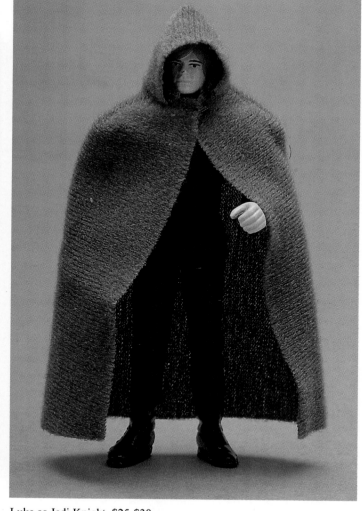

Luke as Jedi Knight, $25-$30 as
shown. *Courtesy of Play With This.*

Klaatu, $6-$8 as
shown. *Courtesy
of Play With This.*

NEW 12" FIGURES for 1980

ITEM	LMC	MIP
Boba Fett	$145	$345
IG-88	$275	$600

ACCESSORIES	LMC	MIP
Imperial Attack Base	$25	$95
Ice Planet Hoth	$55	$160
Tauntaun Solid Belly	$25	$65
Tauntaun Slit Belly	$20	$50
Twin Pod Cloud Car	$45	$85
Imperial Transport (non-talking)	$35	$95
Snow Speeder	$45	$85
ESB Mini-Acessories, each	$9	$19
MCL-3, INT-4,CAP-2,MTV-7, PDT-8, Radar Laser Cannon, Tripod Laser Cannon, and Vehicle Maintenance		
Jedi mini-accesories, each	$9	$18
AST-5,ISP-6,		
Desert Sail Skiff and Endor Forest Ranger		
Star Destroyer	$35	$145
Turret and Probot Set	$45	$125
Slave 1	$45	$95
Battle Damaged X-Wing	$35	$95
Scout Walker	$25	$65
Rebel Transport	$36	$95
Speeder Bike	$15	$33
Y-Wing	$55	$125
Battle Damaged Tie Fighter	$45	$125
B-Wing Fighter	$45	$85
Tie Interceptor	$55	$95
Ewok Assault Catapult	$9	$18

Boba Fett shows off his prize catch, the Han In Carbonite that came with his ship, the Slave-1. *Courtesy of Play With This.*

Detail of Boba's Backpack. *Courtesy of Play With This.*

Ewok Glider	$9	$18
Ewok Battle Wagon	$45	$125
Rancor Monster	$30	$75
One-Man Sand Skimmer	$35	$65
Security Scout Vehicle	$35	$75
Imperial Sniper Vehicle	$40	$80
At-At	$115	$255
AT-AT in Jedi Box $195		
Imperial Shuttle	$175	$350
Tatooine Skiff	$275	$625
Dagobah Playset	$20	$50
Ewok Village	$25	$75
Jabba The Hut Playset	$30	$65
Jabba's Dungeon (Sears Exclusive, a repackaged Droid Factory with Nikto, 8D8, and Klaatu)	$50	$125
Jabba's Dungeon with POTF figures of EV-9D9, Barada, and Amanaman (Be Tee, Ba Teepee)	$200	$320
Cloud City Playset (Sears Exclusive)	$159	$390
Hoth Wampa Monster	$15	$45
Darth Vader Carry Case	$15	$40
Darth Vader Case comes w/figures MIP $350		
C-3PO Collector Case	$15	$25
Chewbacca Bandolier Strap (Carry Case)	$5	$12
JEDI vinyl carrying case	N/A	$78
Laser Rifle carrying case	$14	$25
Display Arena	$50	$100

Many 1970s Star Wars figures and vehicles were reissued in the 1980s. Here's Walrus Man in Empire packaging, $120-$130. *Courtesy of Play With This.*

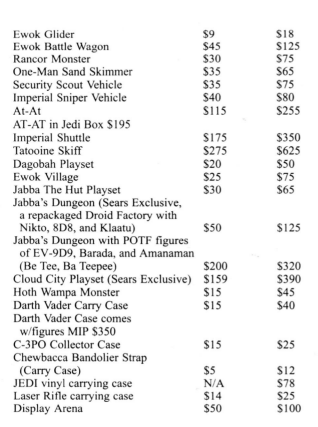

And here's the
original Han Solo on
an Empire card. $250-
$300. *Courtesy of
Play With This.*

Wicket
carded.
*Courtesy of
Play With
This.*

Ree-Yees carded,
$15-$18.
*Courtesy of Play
With This.*

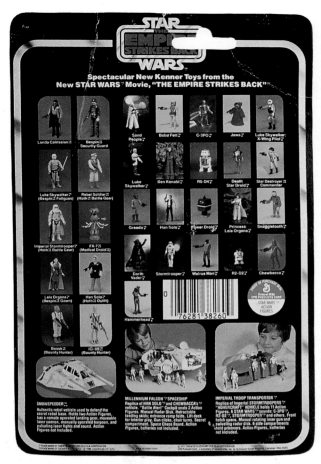

The back of an early Empire card.
Courtesy of Play With This.

They had to abandon individual shots of the figures
as the line expanded. *Courtesy of Play With This.*

By the time the Jedi had their revenge, the back of the
card was pretty crowded. *Courtesy of Play With This.*

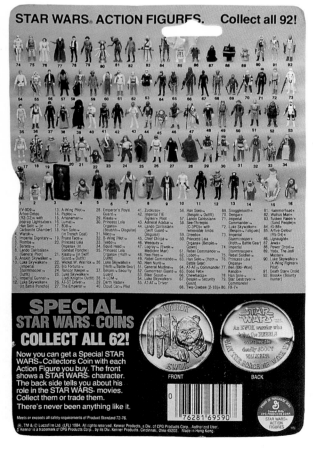

And by the end, well, it just got ridiculous.
Courtesy of Play With This.

STAR WARS
THE POWER OF THE FORCE

SPECIAL
COLLECTORS COIN

Kenner

Han Solo
(In Carbonite Chamber)

Han Solo in Carbonite, not the same as the one that came with Boba's ship. P.O.T.F. version, $200-$225 *Courtesy of Play With This.*

"Get me outta here!" A nice close-up.
Courtesy of Play With This.

A view of the rare display arena...

...and this setup...

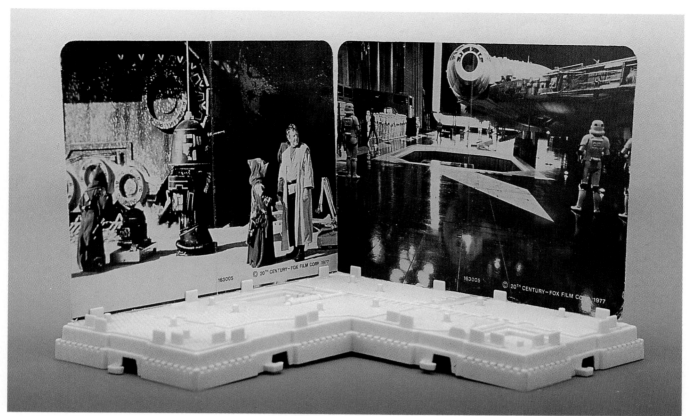

... and this setup...

... and this, $40-$50. *Courtesy of Play With This.*

An impromptu Stormtrooper covention. *Courtesy of Play With This.*

You want your MTV-7, and can have it boxed for a measly $15-$20. *Courtesy of Play With This.*

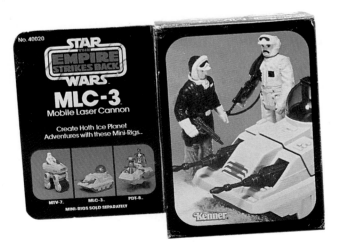

The MLC boxed, $15-$20.
Courtesy of Play With This.

MICRO SERIES

ITEM	LMC	MIP
X-Wing	$29	$60
Imperial Tie Fighter	$29	$69
Death Star Escape	$25	$65
Death Star Compactor	$25	$65
Death Star World	$70	$135
Hoth Wampa Cave	$15	$30
Hoth Turret Defense	$15	$25
Hoth Generator Attack	$15	$25
Hoth Ion Cannon	$20	$40
Hoth World	$65	$95
Bespin Control Room	$15	$35
Bespin Gantry	$15	$35
Bespin Freeze Chamber	$24	$75
Bespin World	$75	$155

DROIDS CARTOON SERIES

ITEM	LMC	MIP
C-3PO	$15	$45
R2-D2	$15	$45
Jann Tosh	$8	$20
Jord Disat	$8	$20
Kea Moll	$8	$20
Kez-Iban	$8	$20
Thall Joben	$8	$20
Uncle Gundy	$8	$15
Tigg Fromm	$25	$60
Sise Fromm	$22	$55
Boba Fett	$35	$200
A-Wing Pilot	$45	$145
A-Wing Ship	$290	$625
Imperial Side Gunner	$15	$50
ATL Interceptor	$10	$35
Mungo Baobab (Not Released)		
Kleb Zellock (Not Released)		
Admiral Screed (Not Released)		

Vlix (Not Released)
Gaff (Not Released)
Mon Julpa (Not Released)
Governor Koong (Not Released)
Jessica Meade(Not Released)

EWOKS CARTOON SERIES

ITEM	LMC	MIP
Wicket	$8	$19
Lady Gorneesh	$8	$16
Logray	$8	$16
King Gorneesh	$8	$15
Dulok Scout	$8	$16
Dulok Shaman	$8	$16
Bondo (Not Released)		
Chituhr (Not Released)		
Weechee (Not Released)		
Paploo (Not Released)		
Morag (Not Released)		
Chief Chirpa (Not Released)		

For some reason, the Imperial Attack Base and Jabba The Hut Dungeon/Droid Factory turn up at flea markets, but rarely does anything else boxed. $75-$95. *Courtesy of Play With This.*

Ha! And here it is, the Jabba The Hut Dungeon, a repackaged Droid Factory. This is the cheap version that does not have Amanaman (ba tee ba teepee). *Courtesy of Play With This.*

Tri-Pod Laser Can-Non requires $15-$20 in Mo-Ney. *Courtesy of Play With This.*

E-e-e-e-eeeWoks! $14-$16.
Courtesy of Play With This.

E-e-e-e-eeeeWoks! $14-$16.
Courtesy of Play With This.

E-e-e-e-eeeeEwoks! $14-$16.
Courtesy of Play With This.

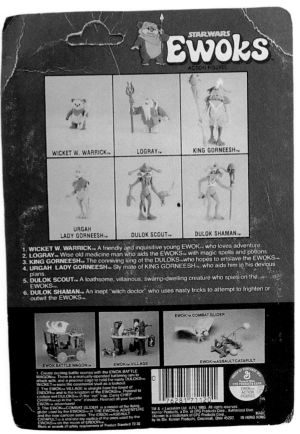

The back of the Ewoks pacakage shows
the goodies. *Courtesy of Play With This.*

Micro X-Wing, $50-$60 boxed.
Courtesy of Play With This.

Hoth Wampa Cave will cost you $25-$30
in Wampa-um. *Courtesy of Play With This.*

Hoth Generator Attack, $20-$25, the kind of set
that was too obscure for a full-size set but perfect
for the Micro series. *Courtesy of Play With This.*

The ascot-blasting Imperial TIE Fighter,
$60-$70 boxed. *Courtesy of Play With This.*

Scenes We'd Like To See: Han miraculously escapes and gets the drop on
Boba. And that's it for this weighty tome of toys! Cowabunga, Begorah!